# NO ONE HAS SEEN IT ALL

*Lessons for Living Well from Nearly a Century of Good Taste*

## BETTY HALBREICH
### with REBECCA PALEY

RUNNING PRESS
PHILADELPHIA

Text copyright © 2025 by Betty Halbreich
Cover copyright © 2025 by Hachette Book Group, Inc.
Foreword copyright © 2025 by Lena Dunham

Hachette Book Group supports the right to free expression and the value of copyright. The purpose of copyright is to encourage writers and artists to produce the creative works that enrich our culture.

The scanning, uploading, and distribution of this book without permission is a theft of the author's intellectual property. If you would like permission to use material from the book (other than for review purposes), please contact permissions@hbgusa.com. Thank you for your support of the author's rights.

Running Press
Hachette Book Group
1290 Avenue of the Americas, New York, NY 10104
www.runningpress.com
@Running_Press

First Edition: April 2025

Published by Running Press, an imprint of Hachette Book Group, Inc.
The Running Press name and logo are trademarks of Hachette Book Group, Inc.

Running Press books may be purchased in bulk for business, educational, or promotional use. For more information, please contact your local bookseller or the Hachette Book Group Special Markets Department at Special.Markets@hbgusa.com.

The publisher is not responsible for websites (or their content) that are not owned by the publisher.

Print book cover and interior design by Susan Van Horn
Cover photos copyright Getty Images

Library of Congress Cataloging-in-Publication Data
Names: Halbreich, Betty, 1927–2024 author. | Paley, Rebecca, author.
Title: No one has seen it all : lessons for living well from nearly a century of good taste / Betty Halbreich with Rebecca Paley.
Description: First edition. | Philadelphia : Running Press, 2025.
Identifiers: LCCN 2024041364 (print) | LCCN 2024041365 (ebook) | ISBN 9780762488568 (hardcover) | ISBN 9780762488575 (ebook)
Subjects: LCSH: Halbreich, Betty, 1927–2024 | Image consultants—United States—Biography. | Clothing and dress. | Fashion. | Beauty, Personal.
Classification: LCC TT505.H24 A3 2025 (print) | LCC TT505.H24 (ebook) | DDC 746.9/2—dc23/eng/20241210
LC record available at https://lccn.loc.gov/2024041364
LC ebook record available at https://lccn.loc.gov/2024041365

ISBNs: 978-0-7624-8856-8 (hardcover), 978-0-7624-8857-5 (ebook)

Printed in the United States of America

LSC-C

Printing 1, 2025

*To my children, grandchildren,
and the one that is coming*

# Contents

*Foreword*..................................vii

*Introduction*..............................xiii

ON WORKING...............................1

ON DRESSING.............................31

ON MANNERS.............................63

ON KEEPING HOUSE ......................79

ON LIVING................................109

ON SOLITUDE............................127

ON AGING................................159

# Foreword

FOR THOSE OF US LUCKY ENOUGH TO HAVE KNOWN BETTY Halbreich, we will never stop hearing her voice in our heads.

In fact, whether you met her once—in a dressing room at Bergdorf's as she walked in with a neat stack of dresses that you should "really give a chance because whatever you're clinging to isn't working"—or you said hello every morning for forty years as she walked purposefully across Madison Avenue—Betty's voice will never leave you. Maybe she sat beside you at a bistro in spring, giving advice with such a vibrato that you caught every word. Maybe she was across the circle in group therapy. Maybe she was your boss, your grandmother, the subject of an interview where you stayed for three hours longer than you needed to. Saying goodbye to Betty was never easy, whether it was at the end of an afternoon or at the end of a lifetime. You wanted—needed—more of what she had to offer. And so you let her take up residence as a voice in your head.

With Betty on the brain, every time you falter at the thing you love, you will be reminded that hard work keeps you young. You will think about the fact that even a woman as imposingly composed as Betty can admit to periods of deep psychic strain, of purposelessness. You will want to rise to greet the vigor of a

FOREWORD

Betty hello, even just in passing on the escalator up from the beauty floor. You will hear her telling you (kindly but firmly) that you really ought to look at getting some slacks that are better tailored to your frame.

I first met Betty in 2013, when an article about her in the *New Yorker* by the legendary Judith Thurman went viral for telling the story of a woman who was working—in the cutthroat world of fashion, no less—well into her eighties. It seemed like it would make an incredible television show, quirky and sweet (two words, I would learn, that were not Betty's forte. Elegant and moral is more the vibe). I also learned—upon our first meeting, and in a profoundly important friendship that has lasted over a decade—that Betty's appeal, her magic, was not in her age. It was, however, in her ability to survive. We tried to write this story of survival—housewife to businesswoman, accessory to doyenne—as a series (although she told us that "nobody wants to watch a show about an eighty-six-year-old lady, not in this America," and, as usual, she was right).

And anyway, Betty has written her own story better than anyone else can—her years as a committed wife and mother, the personal breakdown that followed her marriage's collapse, the rediscovery of self that came with her move into personal shopping, a niche she occupied so well not just because of her fashion sensibility (which was, like all things Betty, singular) but because of her ability to read people like books, to diagnose their needs and what fashion—what *she*—could do to heal them.

FOREWORD

There's a reason she called her shingle Solutions. A prom dress was more than a prom dress. A funeral look for a cheating husband's wake had to express multiple realities. Yes, it was about cut and fit—a sense for which Betty had honed during her daily walks through the store, touching each garment like she was squeezing the shoulder of a new friend—but it was also about storytelling, about the image we project for others and the way we need to feel when we look in the mirror.

Meeting Betty turned out to be a solution for me.

For the past ten years, having a Betty became part of being a Lena. Whether she was extolling the healing power of work and her endless appreciation of the view from her office or counseling me through transitions and heartbreaks with the kind of tough wisdom that makes your face go red (if she didn't know the term "read you for filth," that's because she invented the concept), she was redefining me.

She never gave me a makeover (although we wandered the store together, a treat not only because of her near alphabetical knowledge of its contents but also the greetings she exchanged with every employee, the delight they took in her presence). In truth, she never tried, telling me that it was not her job to dim individuality but to help those who were still looking for their sartorial voice (that being said, she still wanted me in better slacks). But she did, over lengthy meals and transatlantic phone calls, cut to the heart of so many of the things that messed me up and tied me down. Just like she knew how the right dress can change a woman's outlook, she understood—with a surgical precision—the exact types of pain, fear, and shame I felt. She'd felt them too. Over tea in the Bergdorf café, she redressed me spiritually. I always left lighter, as if I'd shed a heavy winter coat and she'd replaced it with a crisp blazer (all of hers were satin with surprising bejeweled details, by her beloved Libertine).

I told her I loved her a lot, and she told me to get it together.

Her writing gives everyone the chance at those long lunches, as if she's offering her readers the same master class in freeing oneself, meeting oneself, shedding the traditional forms of obligation that keep women from rising up to meet their potential but recognizing that it's always something. Betty was wise but never prescriptive. Witty but never cruel. Powerful but vulnerable. A consistent work in progress, even when she'd reached an age where those who remain tend to calcify.

I hope to make it to the peaks Betty scaled—yes, of age, of achievement, but also the peaks of self-actualization. She was the most deeply *herself* woman I have known. She was the guide reminding me that there is always another summit but also telling me to look around. I can't believe how much of the view I would have missed without her. Or how ugly my pants would have been.

The gift of this book is that now, no matter where you are, Betty's voice will never leave you, either.

When I first wrote this foreword, I knew we were saying goodbye—at least in the Western conception of mortality—to Betty. I wrote something I hoped her remarkable children,

FOREWORD

Kathy and John (a powerful, taste-making New York curator and philanthropy advisor, and a volunteer firefighter and EMS worker, respectively, representing the two sides of the coin of Betty's interior life), could read to her out loud that would make clear to her the massive space she occupied in my life but didn't touch on the idea that she was fallible, that she wasn't going to be packing her hand luggage and leaving the hospital and heading back into the sprawling apartment—heavy on the matching florals—that she scrubbed inch by inch until the end of her life. I wrote exclusively using the word "is," hoping that enough present tense could delay the inevitable.

It speaks to the power of someone's life force when, at ninety-six, their death feels like an impossibility. But Betty Halbreich went and did the impossible. And if you know anything about Betty's life, you know that she did the impossible with a shrug.

She started every call with "What am I going to do with you, child?" and ended with "Come by soon, I'm almost [insert upcoming age], you know."

Her last message to me read:

*My Dear So Intelligent Lena,*

*Miss your voice. The book is being edited. It was easy so I hope it's not boring!*

*Also are you ever coming "home" this summer?*

*Love you Anyway,*
*Betty*

xi

FOREWORD

I will miss that escalator up to her office, the royal greetings she received as she mounted the floors from handbags to the designer shoe salon until finally you found yourself on level three: advanced designer collections and Solutions by Betty Halbreich.

I will miss the surprising intensity of her hugs, how her birdlike frame could squeeze harder than men three times her size.

I will miss dialing her 212 number, waiting for that stern "child," and I will miss knowing she is walking toward Fifth Avenue in the morning and away from it at night.

But as long as there is Bergdorf's, as long as there is a Fifth Avenue, as long as there is an isle of Manhattan, and as long as there is a "child," Betty will be here. She's probably passing the hot dog stand right now, with a wave that says, "I have places to be."

There is such beauty to someone dying at the age that dying is meant for, and knowing that they really did it all—the good, the bad, and the glamorous. Everything feels wrong, even though nothing is wrong. This is a celebration, but I cannot help noticing dust everywhere.

Lena Dunham
September 2024

# Introduction

I HAVE ALWAYS WANTED TO REACH OUT TO ALL THE OTHER lonely ones. I'm sure the many who know me would not suspect my true condition. Tucked away in a hidden corner of the third floor of Bergdorf Goodman, where for the last half century I've witnessed the changes in fashion and life as the store's original personal shopper, I've built a career on firm, honest advice. It truly isn't all about clothes. Mostly, I deal in human nature.

When the store originally hired me to run the Geoffrey Beene boutique, I was already forty-nine years old. I had lived an entire life by then, which included a husband, home, children, and even a dog. The kids, by then grown into adults, had left the apartment. So, too, the husband. Only the dog and I remained, and one of us didn't react too well to all the change. I suffered a nervous breakdown and landed in a psychiatric hospital. It was after that when I began working at Bergdorf's. Quite a transition, I'll admit. While I loathed the sales floor (the register and I have never been on friendly terms since I don't add or subtract), I loved helping women look and feel their best. I went to the higher-ups and pitched the idea of starting a personal-shopping service. The rest is history, as they say. Ancient history.

INTRODUCTION

Because I am of the nature that I must keep busy, both physically and mentally, even at ninety-six, I am perceived by most as strong. Oh, how I wish it were true. Some people can't fathom that I've been to the institution and back. While I may be known for my "eye," my head is a little less reliable. I have learned, while still reflecting on the past, to get on with the present. I try very hard not to dwell, because it wouldn't help one bit. To dispel the gloom, each day I say, "Onward!" I have worked hard these past forty-eight years at the store, which has been good to me and, most of all, for me.

In the spring of 2020, a new virus descended on the world, and New York City was quarantined. The store was shuttered, as were schools, banks, museums, Broadway, everything. In the bustling place I've called home ever since leaving my native Chicago more than seventy-five years ago to marry a New Yorker, you could hear a pin drop. Silence was no longer something only for the old.

During those months when only essential workers were allowed to go about their business, I moved about my overly large apartment like a ghost. The building I have lived in for nearly as long as I have been in Manhattan emptied out as its residents fled for second homes and freer climes. By May, it seemed as though the doormen and I were the only ones left. They grew nervous if they didn't see me in the lobby collecting my mail or standing out on Park Avenue for a little sun on my face.

INTRODUCTION

I had never been so lonely in my whole life, and that is saying quite a lot, because for almost a half century I have lived alone. In my relentless neatness—I can always find a dust ball somewhere—I have come to accept loneliness as the price paid for a life on my terms. I can fluff up one chair cushion each evening, but not two. An "outsider" would drive me up the wall. Selfish in a way, but on the other hand it is my survival kit.

The pandemic lockdown was different; I felt the whole world had abandoned me.

One day, I picked up the pen and put it to the legal pad. I began by describing my observations of such a strange and scary time when it appeared that everyone, apart from the doormen and me, had deserted the Upper East Side. How desolate the streets were. Writing helped to ward off the fear and loneliness that come from utter isolation. When I could no longer bear to describe my daily chats with the masked doormen or people's newfound obsession with cooking that I heard about over countless phone calls, memories began to enter into my daily legal pad entries. Dinners eaten alone as a child, opulent table arrangements I created for dinner parties as a newlywed, entering the working world in middle age: a lot of feelings accumulate over ninety-six years. Initially, I wrote to soothe my nerves and fill those long empty days. Never did I imagine offering it as a balm for others.

Although I have long since returned to my nine-to-five at the store and the pandemic has receded from public memory, I have not missed a day of writing since I began. The yellow legal pads, covered by my left hand, continue to grow and grow until my basket literally overfloweth.

Writing has become important to my daily life, a practice that I enjoy and have never once felt an effort to complete. It takes me back to my teens when I kept a diary (locked up in a drawer away from anyone's eyes). I'm very fussy about the pen situation. It must glide easily over the page, or I lose my thoughts. This may seem silly as most do not write in pen and ink but rather computer, computer! I have never touched that particular machine, nor the cell phone, and I never shall.

That I'd never miss a single day of writing would not have occurred to me when I began, but in retrospect it makes a lot of sense. While I am disciplined (to a fault, I might add), the practice goes beyond force of habit. Despite my appearance as "put together," I am probably the frailest person I know, worrying that catastrophe and chaos lurk around every corner. That is why I started to write; I didn't want fear to drag me down.

I don't want to sound like a malcontent. In some ways I am. I have known devastating unhappiness along with loneliness, not to mention physical problems—everything most people go through in this life. From this writing each day, however, I have let go of so many irritating things. This sounds simplistic but by digging deeper I have found some sort of peace. Writing is an outlet for so many feelings, good and bad. It eases the tensions and also the quietness. Ending every day fulfilled and

INTRODUCTION

accomplished by simply putting pen to paper, I want to offer up some sort of thank-you, a prayer perhaps.

People—friends, my children even—applaud me for the diligence and commitment to my legal pads. But no one fully understands the compulsion that arises, regardless of how I feel mentally or physically. It is as if my pen, or "wand," were my director.

I have had many lives. I can still remember being a frightened young bride from Chicago arriving in New York City, where I raised two children, split up from my husband, Sonny, suffered a nervous breakdown, and reinvented myself as a workingwoman and a weekend housewife to my friend Jim, with whom I never fully merged lives but spent wonderful years enjoying each other's company in the country from Friday to Sunday. When he passed away, I had to reorganize my life yet again and became the lone person I am today.

I have come to understand that my perspective is of interest. This is mainly from all the people who approach me on the street, in letters and emails, even outside the ladies' room at work. They are all types—young and not so young, men and women, fashion lovers and farmers—and they are looking for, if not advice, then a different point of view. In this dizzying time with little direction, many wonder what is to come and what will become of them.

At ninety-six, I am in a *very* exclusive group. I don't think a great deal about my age, but when I look at the long list of doctor appointments facing me, then I know for sure just how old I am. The head is still working but the feet and legs don't often agree. My withered hands will go before my brain.

However, old age has its advantages. We hopefully possess an important outlook by virtue of the fact that we've been alive for quite a while. Perhaps some of us in old age become a bit wiser; we have more time to acquire the advantage. Look at all the things we have learned and the great amount of information we have to pull from. I won't say this club doesn't have its frightening bits, but I'm more appreciative than ever that I am on my feet and for the day ahead.

I have learned that combatting fear and loneliness is a challenge, not of just old age but any age. Although I'm a pessimist by birth, I am one who believes in change, in part because I have experienced it in myself, albeit kicking and screaming. This is the perspective I want to share with the other lonely ones out there—and there are many of you. Until you take your last breath, it is possible to find new, happier, more fulfilling paths.

Between these two covers is a simple tale of an old woman writing thoughts and, most importantly, feelings. I know my views will not be to everyone's taste. (I am apparently the last person living who refuses to wear shorts, use a cell phone, or work from home; I don't believe in any of it.) Take what you like and leave the rest. This is my time to give back. That I truly believe in. For in the end, when I have departed, I do not seek grand accolades. Rather, I wish to be thought of as a person who was open to those who needed me.

I hope reading these thoughts will help others as much as writing them down helped me. My one fear in all the years I have been writing on my legal pads is that one day I will have nothing to put down on paper. I cannot allow that to happen. Even if I only write down what I ate for lunch, I will hold on to the pen and paper until I dry up.

# ON WORKING

# Busy Is So Frustratingly Wonderful

THERE IS NOTHING LIKE A BUSY DAY IN THE OFFICE.

I come to the store early each day before it is open. There are very few persons about as I walk the floors to see what's new—maybe the man with the vacuum. I love the quiet of the early morning. Quiet is never boring at the office; it's a peaceful retreat before the busyness of the day begins.

If I do run into someone, I throw out a one-liner for all to smile at. The other morning, around 8:30 a.m., I was making my rounds and saw the building's painters, three great guys. One was just a kid when he came to the store twenty years ago. So many people have been working at the store many years: employees of the alteration department, the window dressers, the cleaning group, security, it goes on and on. In a strange way, Bergdorf Goodman is a family.

The other two painters have been patching the walls of the store even longer than the "kid." Think about it: there is always change going on in construction and decor. Walls come and go, as do boutiques with famous, costly names above their entrances. The beauty of the store alone lends itself to opulence. There isn't another one like it. With one side facing the Plaza Hotel and the Pulitzer Fountain, the store holds the whole fifty-eighth block at its command and in lovely taste. I cannot imagine it changed or demolished. All the people who have owned it in the past, and there have been many in my forty-eight-year tenure, have kept the store in pristine and tasteful shape. I am not a prophet but believe it will remain that way.

In those quiet early hours of the morning, before I begin my day with clients, I often go back into the past. Today, while walking the sales floor, I imagined my father, Harry, doing the same so many years ago. I remember him as a tough boss, who put in many hours as president of the Chicago department store Mandel Brothers. Those were hands-on retail days. He never, ever complained; he loved his work. I had to wait for Daddy to come home to have dinner, only to often sup without him when it got too late. He was totally engrossed, and I suspect rarely looked at his watch, which would have told him it was time to lock up. He was admired in the business not only for his work ethic but also for his innovations and treating his employees with the greatest respect. His secretary Marie—who stayed with him from early on, through all his career changes, until he died—was so intensely dedicated to him that she regularly placed flowers on his grave after he passed. While Daddy was still alive, she kept the same long hours as my father. A life outside of work did not exist for Marie, who was loathed by my mother.

This is ancient history, almost literally. Still, I think of my father while walking the floor and wonder, "Would he approve of the job I have done?" He was always so proud of me, even when I wasn't doing anything.

Being idle is no longer available to me. I am very uncomfortable not doing a job. Work has become the most important thing in my life. When I am working, I feel, in one word, safe.

On Mondays, I go back to work with glee! I'm overjoyed to return to my desk and chair, and to my window in the office, which, for me, is a doorway to the world. From the glorious double-hung window I am able to care for the horse and carriages that enter Central Park, worrying for them when it is too hot *and* too cold. I love seeing groups of young people being escorted to the park with front and back "captains." During the holiday season, the Christmas trees around the fountain are extravagantly glittery. My special favorite view is at twilight, when hundreds of swallows seem to come out of nowhere and flock to the trees right outside the office. Their silhouettes make beautiful patterns against dusk, and as quickly as it occurs, it ends when darkness falls.

As I look around my office of forty-some years, I gaze at some of the memorabilia. There are pictures of my family on my desk, none too current, as they do not enjoy being photographed. The photograph of my beloved dog, Max, who stayed with me through some of the worst times, has faded with the sun bright off Central Park. I will never eat the chocolate gun Joan Rivers sent me after spending a day at the store when I was distressed. There are five individual metal fingers, their nails polished, from someone unknown. One finger arrived at the office each day for five days. A mystery, never solved. There are magazines (now defunct) in which I appeared, dressing clients or giving advice to those in need, and many books written by people I have known, many gone, and all so very important to me. My most favorite memento, however, is a painting of the view from my desk, out the window, of the Grand Army Plaza fountain and horse and carriages. It was given to me when I published my memoir, *I'll Drink to That*. I treasure it and always will.

People admire me for continuing to hold down a nine-to-five at ninety-six years old. They do not realize; it is a magnificent tool in my day-to-day existence. We all wish to stay at a certain age. No one likes to feel they are becoming old. My resistance to this is working.

For me, a day of looking, trying on, working the floor stimulates the body as well as the brain. Preferring to walk the floors and pull items alone—where my vision is guided by the patron—I was the only shopper who didn't use her assistant as the "holder of the pull." If my back hadn't given in, I would have never given it up. I can't run, carry, do what I once did physically five days a week like I used to. Does this mean I am getting ready for the end of my career? It is a brutal thing for me even to consider. I am still productive at work, even if there is a bit of coasting on my reputation, akin to hanging your name over the entrance to the office. People do recognize me and identify me with the store, even if I've never reached out for fame. Celebrity is fleeting, coming one day and then mostly disappearing until the death notice might entice it to rise once again.

My thrust is not to lose who I am, who I was when I started, a listener above all else. I have never cared what the client purchases in terms of the dollar amount; the interaction is what I crave. People present the gift of communication, conversations about gardening, vacations, family, and on and on. You cannot pay for that kind of deviation from one's own thoughts. The hours fly by. Sure, there are always problems, but they are usually solvable and don't include health issues!

In the office, even if there are no clients, there are always the plants waiting for me to water them. "Welcome!" they seem to say. My orchids survive and bloom on the windowsill. I've always had plants at work. It brings a bit of the outside in. I love greenery, really anything that grows, as did my mother. She, too, tended to myriad flowers and plants in the bookstore she ran at the end of her life.

My mother, Carol, had a sense of humor, and a caustic one at that. A Fanny Brice lookalike, she often made fun of herself for a laugh. Also like Fanny Brice, Mother had great taste in clothing but never made it a focus. Throughout her life, she was a tremendous reader. My indelible memory of her is her reading in bed, or on the couch—anywhere with a book in hand. She opened Oak Street Book Shop, an old three-story walk-up brownstone, after the death of my father. My mother, who idolized him, completely changed when he passed away in his early sixties. Father had a memory bank that was startling. You couldn't catch him unawares on anything—religious, political, or economic. They argued but always made up. A good couple, they kept each other interested. The Oak Street bookstore saved her inner life after my father died. She became a stronger, more confident person. All of her being was in the bookstore.

Persons familiar with owning a bookstore will tell you they really don't make money. If so, very little. That worried her. She became fraught when business was slow. It truly terrified her. There were many bumpy days when she didn't sell one book, even though she had a knack for selling. "You could sell old clothes for new," I often said to her. She could pitch a book like no one I have ever come across. She couldn't possibly have read all the books she professed to know about, but she was not unlike a librarian, knowledgeable and believable.

The value of the bookstore was to be found not only in her "money books," the ledgers where she kept track of her sales. Mother created a new persona: an independent woman. She did most everything herself at work (so many things besides making an actual sale). With the coffee machine going, she offered coffee cake to her favorite customers. On a shelf next to the register were coffee cups engraved with the names of these men. (Yes, they were all men. Not a single woman earned a cup on that shelf.) They were from television, the arts, big business, all varieties. The policeman on the block often appeared for his cup of coffee and discussion. I always suspected he preferred the bookshop to his beat. He kept a very watchful eye toward Mother.

When I visited from New York, I sat on the only chair near the register. There was a great deal to absorb in the people alone. I observed how my mother totally immersed herself in her favorite customers' lives. And believe me, they confided a lot! Occasionally, out of the blue, someone who was young when a parent took them to the bookstore to meet my mother will get in touch with me to describe the very large impression she made. It is a thrill and makes me very proud.

I wonder what my mother would think of all that has passed in my life. After my marriage broke up, she wanted me to find some well-to-do man, a "country club" fellow, and to start over. Perhaps she wished for me to be taken care of, believing that was the easiest way. I didn't follow her advice. I went the same route she took—working and building some sort of reputation.

On quiet days in my own office, I think about Mother and reflect on how I followed in her footsteps. What I've done for the past forty-eight years at the store is not unlike what she did in her shop. I've learned so very much about people over the years, becoming a psychologist without the degree, as did she. I believe my mother would be so proud of me and say, "See, Betty, I always told you that you were smart!"

While the bookstore nourished her soul, it also took a great deal out of her physically. She usually had only one part-time young man helping her unpack new books, stack them, and run errands. I have a photo of her from the day she had to close the bookstore. Surrounded by her dearest friends—Bruce Gregga, an interior designer, and his partner, Victor Skrebneski, a one-of-a-kind photographer—she looks more than sad. Her expression is rather angry, like the world is coming to an end. It was for her. Soon after, she took to her bed and saw no one. My children and I were the only exceptions. I always felt she wished for the end after that, which makes me sad to think about.

I inherited much from my mother. I, too, built a reputation. However, I do not dwell upon it. The reason being, I never feel I am finished. I must not dwell only on what was and instead try to look forward a bit. There is a department that is still functioning, and as long as I am sitting at my desk, a presence, it will persist.

Believe me, I'm not through yet. Every day, thoughts run through my head on how to bring new things to the store's clientele. For example: Why shouldn't we have a cooking department on the gift floor? How about a small space for white shirts for all seasons? The inventive part of my brain is still active and keeps me going. I so want to finish my career with something new added.

In reality, I have not given any thought to the day I hang up the gloves. I imagine it will come upon me swiftly. In fact, I'll probably be taken out feetfirst. I am grateful to my wonderful office and a job situation I have reached after beginning from nothing such a lifetime ago. So many tell me how unusual I am to still be working. I smile to myself and think, "If you only had known my mother!"

There is a safe harbor in sameness. From the moment I get up, I have my routine: make the bed, put the kettle on, get dressed, eat breakfast, read the paper, and head to work. There is no deviating, no matter what I feel that day, which makes it easier to pull it together, even when I don't think I can, and open the door to this little office.

*Your* routine, no matter how routine, is a good thing.

# Work from Home Is Not in My Vocabulary

DURING THE PANDEMIC, WORKING AT HOME WAS A LIFELINE for many. It allowed some sort of commerce to proceed without exposing oneself to the "plague." Of course, I don't use the computer. But even if I did, I couldn't operate my business cloistered in my apartment sending photos back and forth. No, no! Mine is a face-to-face or at least my-face-to-their-body operation. I had to come back to the office, or there would have been no office to come back to! Almost as soon as the store reopened, before the vaccine was available, I was back in my perch overlooking the Pulitzer Fountain, the Plaza Hotel, and my corner of Central Park. And I was glad of it.

I know there were those who wondered why I was not more housebound. I was, after all, a ninety-three-year-old in a public place as a virus raged that felled those my age and younger! Nearly every single one of my family, friends, and clients had fled New York City altogether. They thought I was cuckoo to return to work in a store. I would have gone cuckoo if I hadn't.

To rise in the morning, dress for work, and spend a day mingling, talking, and learning gives one purpose. I like to see my security people who hold the door open for me at 8:30 a.m., then say hello to the guys in the delivery room dealing with all those online returns. I walk through the store and chat up the early birds who put it to rights: the cleaners, those in the stockroom, and my managers. To be with others is the very best balm for all. You may come into work with bad thoughts, but after talking with others find we are all rowing in the same boat. The paddling may still be hard, but there is comfort in knowing you are not alone.

Not even a virus that attacked the elderly could keep me away. My brilliant and careful assistant, Maria, and I were masked. Very few entered the office (very few were around to enter), and those who did usually didn't do more than grace the hallway door. That is how we managed to go to work, which I feel so deeply about. Even though I could see very few people in person, we stayed busy, keeping on top of what merchandise arrived at the store and calling clients with anything that might appeal in the moment (mainly sweaters; we sold oh so many sweaters).

It's been years since New Yorkers were ordered by the mayor and governor to stay at home, and, still, many people continue to quarantine. They call it "working from home." I don't approve of it. It is, in a word, insular. Sitting in your kitchen, listening to your dog bark, staring at your furniture, you are surrounded with all sorts of things other than work, which can't be as productive. It can't be. They aren't just a distraction. They are also other versions of *you* staring back at yourself. To spend all one's time in a world of one's own making is enough to send anyone to the institution.

I do not believe this "new world" is a healthy environment. The workplace is a way to mingle with people other than our relatives, get outside oneself, learn new things, and see how others go about a task. For the young, it's important to find mentors or those you admire. For everyone, including the not as young like me, the office is a welcome diversion from home: a reason to shower and dress, pack a lunch of leftovers, shut the door on chores, hear stories and thoughts that aren't your own. In short order, get outside yourself.

*A workplace family is so important. You do not have to love them, or even like them. But they are company!*

# We Are All Salesmen of Sorts

MY MARIA, MY EVER-SO-SMART ASSISTANT AND ALTER EGO, walked into the office, where I was turning the plants on the sill of the window overlooking a frigid Central Park.

"Betty, the store is letting people go," she said.

I was alarmed, but where is my reality factor? Why wouldn't employees be terminated?

People had been calling for days after reading in the newspaper that Neiman Marcus, the store's parent company, was filing for bankruptcy. After over forty years with the company, I cannot remember how many large companies have come to our rescue. This time, however, there was no cavalry riding in at the last minute. Bankruptcy was declared loud and clear, leading many to wonder if Bergdorf Goodman would shut its doors. We are unique, at least in the beauty of this gem of a building on Fifth Avenue. Yes, from the packages I see as I walk into the service entrance every morning, people want to press a computer button more than they want to shop in the store. But would they dare close a museum?

For better or worse, we live in a selling culture. Whether you are trading in designer clothes or vegetable peelers, this is how business runs: not how we want it to, but how the client wills it so. Who knows this better than me? You can spend hours with a client, being very professional, think all has gone well after she has purchased a number of special items she looks and, just as importantly, *feels* special in. Then lo and behold! After the garments are delivered to the client's residence—and maybe shown to a husband who poo-poos them (usually because of the price)—one finds a return of those "special" pieces back at the office. Returns after all the long, hard work are difficult to swallow.

As the world continues to turn, so do the ways in which the customer purchases and what they want to purchase. At this time, when everyone is enamored with the computer screen, the huge online retailers are the only marketplaces whose business is booming. Everyone is trying to invent or just reinvent something to draw the customer back into the fold. I shudder as I watch the poor salespeople on the floor of the store use their cell phones to get a client interested.

Upon learning of the bankruptcy, my initial concern was for Maria, my right arm, clever and personable, a lawyer in disguise. It was only later in the morning that I realized I was worried about myself. Some might assume that I was frightened of losing the prestige or relevance my gilded perch affords. They would be wrong. I have had one job for forty-eight years, the same plants in the window and pictures on my desk all that time. Without it, where would I go from 8:15 a.m. to 5:15 p.m.

five days a week? I am hopeless without structure and purpose to the day.

At 4 p.m. (near what I once called the "vodka hour"), the phone rang at Maria's desk. She learned from management that her job was saved. What about the people in the stockroom? Or the security guards who hold the door open for me in the morning? How were they and their families? I refrained from talking and listened. I cop out at times like this and don't retain what I don't want to hear.

I, too, have my own methods of invention, but I find my core process remains relevant as the world turns. As a distraction while doing fittings, I talk to the client about "the outside world," usually nothing to do with clothes and dressing. Very often this gives me an insight to the "real" person. My belief is that clothes have a great deal to do with one's personality. After all, they're your outer skin, or the costume you show the world. If you learn about what people do in their real life and how, you can figure out their style. I get to know my clients quite well, not because I hope to upsell them but because I'm genuinely curious and interested. Learning what makes someone tick is one of my favorite aspects of the job. It's the therapy bit.

No matter your profession, if you take a true interest in your client—not just transactionally but human to human—you will reap rewards. They might not always be financial. There are intellectual and spiritual gifts to be had as well. Here is my advice: first and foremost, be honest—that is the motto I live by, my North Star. Also, challenge yourself—try new products or change your approach according to the client. Above all, do not get bored of what you do. That is the demise of selling.

NO ONE HAS SEEN IT ALL

# Beware of the Salesperson's Taste

IN MY LIFE, THERE IS A VERY FINE LINE BETWEEN FRIENDS and clients. It is impossible to be in business for half a century without a little blurring between the two. My solution to this, how I keep the two separate, is to be completely (some might say "brutally") honest in the way I sell. I am what they term in the business a "soft sell": my goal is not to make a sale at any cost.

This is an example of how I have always worked and will always work. The other day I sold a new Alexander McQueen jacket, which came with matching pants, but I discouraged my client from buying the pants as the jacket looked better on its own. Most "clerks" would not even think of doing this, turning down a sale! At least I can go home at night without an ounce of guilt.

I've always maintained a take-it-or-leave-it attitude toward selling. From my very first day on the job, I have believed that honesty is the easiest way to do business and live with yourself. What I have discovered all these years later is that with this attitude comes a lasting trust. I think of it as money in the bank. Yes, people come to me thinking they need one thing and often end up with something completely different. But even if it isn't something they would have found or picked out for themselves walking through the store on their own, it is always a piece they wind up truly liking.

Do not let a salesperson unduly influence you on what to buy. Their choices are sometimes predicated on what adds to their paycheck. You—not they—are the one making the purchase. Do so with your own mind and taste.

> I do not want to be known as that pushy woman. I want to be known for taste and decorum.

# A Bit About Recognition

I AM AWARE THAT WHEN NEW CLIENTS ARRIVE, THEY COME in scared to death of me. I actually have to beckon them to come in at all! They stand timidly at the threshold of my door, barely able to cross until I lighten the mood by throwing out a sample of the one-liners I'm famous for. "It's your money we're spending." Or some such.

I'm treated with some sort of dignity. Even stylists, not usually known for their passivity, stand back before they enter my office. Age is a factor. Many wonder out loud why I'm still sitting here. My occupational longevity is unheralded in current times. I also like to think my taste plays a part.

It is curious that there are so many people who know me by reputation—even young ones, whose interest in a ninety-six-year-old I can't fathom. I've truly never strived to see my name in lights. Rather, the reverse; I find recognition nervous-making. I loathe having my picture taken so much that I'd destroy any camera if I could.

Whatever the reason for the deference, everyone thinks I am an extraordinarily strong woman, when in truth I am quite a fearful human. So naturally frightened am I that for many years,

I didn't speak. This was before I ever imagined having a career. I never went after attention. Actually, it really intimidated me. I was anxious about walking into a room of people and shied away from large events. I don't dance and often felt clumsy or uncomfortable. When I had to participate in social situations as a young woman, I usually eyed the room to find the least conspicuous hiding place. My husband, I recollect, often pushed me forward into groups.

Then I came here, to work, and found my voice. It's developed over the years so that now being verbal is my stick and my wand. As it turns out, I am not a shy person, and today I stand up and forward to converse with all—whether I know them or not. My business has brought that out in me.

I feel very fortunate that so many persons have walked through my office door. That would have been more than enough for me, but many have also come bearing gifts. Over the years, I have been gifted anything and everything from cookies flown in from Germany to luxurious bags of cloth embroidered with my initials. Not to mention all the beautiful, extraordinary books I have received, enough to fill a small library. There is an early book from the makeup artist Bobbi Brown with a photograph of me unsuccessfully trying to look at ease. Every book in my office, even the cookbooks, have a personal connection: the biography on Isak Dinesen by Judith Thurman, the brilliant writer who profiled me for the *New Yorker*; Melissa Rivers's book about her mother and my dear client Joan; Emily Spivack's *Worn in New*

*York*, which includes my favorite Jean Muir dress; Patricia Volk's *Shocked*; and my dear Geoffrey Beenes, including the Sotheby's catalog from his estate's auction. My most precious book is a copy of Willa Cather's *My Ántonia*, lifted from some library in Floral Park by Michael Vollbracht, an artist, designer, and fine human, who inscribed it:

*For Betty*
*Sorry not a first edition*
*X Michael*

Circumstances, fortunes, even temperaments are subject to change. Recognition, respect, reputation—these can take a long time to develop, so be patient, hardworking, and believe.

*Whenever I meet someone who says "are you....? which is quite often and most usually when I am in the Bathroom of the store - I answer, I aren't !!*

# I Have Always Preferred My Own Identity

I'M AWARE I'M BEST KNOWN AS "THAT PERSONAL SHOPPER at Bergdorf's," and that is all well and good. However, I do want people to know there is more to that person.

I have always tried to live two lives. One at the store, five days a week, and the other during evenings and weekends at home. It is easy now at my age. I have excuses. Early on it was not as easy, but I never wanted extracurricular activities related to my job and the store. Unusual in my industry, I am told. I have a certain curtain I pull down between the two. If people in a social situation try to engage me in clothing or beauty talk, I quickly dissuade them. If I can't, I give them about five minutes before I hightail it out.

Despite my attempts at separation, I have often been mentioned in the same breath as Bergdorf Goodman. That can be a good thing in many respects; I'm appreciative of what the store brings to me. I have met so many smart and interesting characters, made lifelong friendships, and mentored young people who have gone on to successful careers. No matter how many times I am interviewed by the press or stopped in the store, each day I remind myself I am a glorified salesperson.

The store is a large part of who I am, but I have always preferred my own identity—Betty. No matter what and who occupies your life, reserve a bit that is all you.

# Be of Service

EVER SINCE I STARTED MY INSTAGRAM ACCOUNT, I CANNOT believe the requests I have received for advice. Perhaps I might go online and institute a "Dear Betty" service. I am positive I would be inundated with questions, but I'd probably end up making up the answers. With so many young persons out of work and scrambling, I suggest they diversify, try new avenues, even if they feel they are overqualified. The job market today, no matter what field, is very tenuous. Frightening. In every case, there is a great deal to be learned. Only at my age do I realize that setbacks can be an advantage.

My office has always been a problem-solving place. During all my years here, I have liked helping people—career woes, family frustrations, poor health, and a million other bothersome situations. Helping someone else has always helped me. It is a blessing in that you forget your own problems. By the time I've finished the task of helping someone, often I feel much better within. I successfully built an entire department on such self-therapy.

I do like people, all different kinds and types. My mother's child yet again. Of all those I have been willing and able to assist, perhaps my favorite are young people starting out in their careers. Jewelers just beginning, clothing designers, artists—I

NO ONE HAS SEEN IT ALL

love, *love* that part of my job and life. Being at Bergdorf Goodman does help with an introduction. I am good at putting people together. In another life I would have had an employment agency. I like anything different and eclectic, including personalities. Isaac Mizrahi and Michael Kors were a few of the young unknowns who passed through my door. Last week, while searching for Christmas items, I crashed right into Michael on the gift floor. We stood right in the middle aisle, blocking others from passing, and talked about the past and his current life. You would have thought we were related and hadn't seen each other in years.

I picked up my dear, most-handsome young wonder person on the third floor of the store. Edward Bess was nineteen years old then, dressed head to toe in black, with short hair blown and brushed into a pompadour. Different and dramatic, he was stationed on the cosmetic floor, standing all day with a display that housed lipsticks. When you have a good eye, you can find treasures anywhere.

Many years later, he still wears mostly black, but his hair is ever so long, almost to his waist. Now in his thirties, he runs a cosmetics empire and is one of my dearest friends. We speak every day at three o'clock. Because he has a wonderful mother, father, and siblings, I figure I'm his surrogate granny. For my most recent birthday, he made me pea soup. No matter, we share so much. I am as proud of him and his success as if he were one of my own. I wait each day for the three o'clock ring and "Hi, Betty!" How fortunate I am.

I feel the most when needed. If I believe in you, I jump at the chance to help you pursue whatever you show or ask me. I plunge in and try to put people together for the project. Example: a renowned photographer did the most extraordinary book—people who inhabit the jungles of Colombia, remote places, scenery. I introduced him to an extraordinary art collector, originally from Venezuela. They hit it off like gangbusters. I wasn't finished. A friend and client of many years owns a lovely bookstore on Long Island, well-known and thriving. She ordered some books for the store and herself.

I cannot capture how this fulfills me; when you believe in something, whatever it might be, sharing it with others makes it even more wonderful. When one shares, the return is usually twofold. In the process you also tend to learn so much. If you are not successful, which may happen, there is usually good reason. So try again. It is probably the most gratifying thing I attempt, and with no fear or worries that I might fail.

# Make Your Workplace Somewhere Worth Visiting

I AFFECTIONATELY CALL MY OFFICE THE DO DROP INN because, although I take clients only by appointment, people are always arriving unannounced to see if the doctor is in. Never mind clothing, these "visitors" are always welcome to come and sit on my loveseat.

I hail from a long line of gatherers. My mother drove us over to my grandmother's most every weekend to join the ladies who came for coffee and cake. I loved the aunties, who fussed over me, exclaiming how pretty I was (I didn't believe them), until I was asked to go play in another room, so they could continue on with their gossip. Walls were no match for my big ears, which picked up every word of their conversations, usually about their married children and, of course, their spouses. Some of the talk was cruel—I understood beyond my years—as it went to the heart of their dissatisfaction.

My father was big on inviting strays to holidays at our house when I was a child. He thought nothing of asking those dealing with a difficult situation to stay for a week until they got everything under control—and often their stay stretched into a month. That was a nice, warm, fun part of growing up.

All these scenarios turned me into a good listener as a grown-up: First as a wife and mother when the children were still at home and at every-night dinners there was always enough for the unexpected guest who arrived at an apartment lit up with action and the yapping of our beloved dog, Max. Then as a workingwoman in an office where so many persons, even men, seem comfortable to come and chat about the world, family, all different things. I think often of my mother and the bookstore when I reflect on the ambience it took years for me to accomplish in my own office. It is she reincarnated, and I must say it makes me happy.

Visitors seem to be the new game in town. I am receiving them more frequently. Some come from far into my past, wanting to catch up and see if I'm still alive; others are new and hoping to hear my story. I must say I do feel honored to be surrounded by so many different types from walks of life that intrigue me and remove me from what could be a very insular existence. Their stories are a healthy distraction. Becoming too intense about your business and engrossed in a single activity is not the way to live.

I do wonder how management perceives the department, particularly when the socializing takes over. No one is more surprised than I that I've become a tourist attraction. Some days, the office is a salon rather than a place to purchase clothes. I'm so appreciative of the heads poking around the hall to the office, but they don't pay my salary. However, forty-eight years after I started, I am sitting in the same chair, receiving those who come to visit.

The most remarkable part of any job, and one that you cannot put in the money book, is the attachment persons have to you. I have never gone out of my way to hold on to anyone, but I count my blessings when they want to be a part of my life.

# ON DRESSING

# Rarely Does Anyone Know Their Right Size

RARELY DOES ANYONE KNOW THEIR RIGHT SIZE. EVERY designer cuts a dress using different proportions. It's inevitable that you will wear a variety of sizes. Yet this is most difficult to get across to a client. They resist certain sizes. It is a true mental thing, and I become the clothes doctor in these cases. Perhaps my inability to cope with numbers has served me well when this happens. The label may say size 12 but can a size 12 fit inside? I gauge the length of the sleeve, look under the armholes, plumb the space for the bosom. While I never learned to sew (I always wanted to), I understand structure and can tell the fit of a dress before it goes on the body. However, most people cannot. If a garment you love is a little snug in a 12, go up a size. Cut out the tag if it bothers you that much! You are still you, a human being, not a number.

# The Mirror Is Not Your Friend

SO MANY ANXIETIES APPEAR ONCE A PERSON IS CLOISTERED in the dressing room. The three-way mirror is a true revelation to all. It is the human condition that we never see all of ourselves. Even though we see others both coming toward and leaving us, we tend to forget the backs of our own heads and bodies. As someone who wears honesty as a mantle, I insist on my clients being aware of the entire reflection. The mirror is a point of contention, a frightening but necessary tool.

Most clients arrive not liking themselves—*really* not liking themselves. They don't like their bodies or their clothes. Maybe they don't like their hair or their face. I move the client and the mirrors in the dressing room to show all the different sides of the garment and the human inside. Staring at themselves, they become completely mute, dare I say, mirror-struck. It is uncomfortable. They do a lot of fixing. I can relate; I don't like looking at myself either.

Mirrors have never been my friend. Generally, I have a disdain for them. It is quickly on with the makeup in my dark bathroom early in the morning. Often that's the last time I will look at my reflection until day's end. When you do what I do, there is little time to worry about oneself. Let the clients do that. Sometimes, however, I will look in the office mirror while adding more lipstick after lunch. My own mother was known for putting on her lipstick without any mirror. It was fun to watch, a miracle in makeup. I have no such talent; when I try, I catch my image in the mirror and I am aghast. I must run back to the ladies' room, four floors above my office, just to powder my nose, fluff the hair, and add the lipstick.

Without any reflection, true beauty is impossible. I have always felt that looking honestly at one's accomplishments is like seeing oneself in a mirror. I am not talking about becoming so imbued with one's image that one loses sight of reality. Taking stock of my achievements is an antidote to the restless need to achieve more.

In simple terms, I like making people look good, so pretty that when they see themselves in the dressing room mirror, a smile crosses their face. They turn to me for approval and the lack of fear invades the fitting. Now two people are happy.

*I am of the NEW School - do whatever makes you comfortable. Honestly though, I cannot keep up with all the different solutions available these days.*

# Buy Better

THE LONG FORTY-EIGHT YEARS I HAVE WORKED HAVE ALL been different. There have been a great many changes in the store, and not only in the merchandise. When I first began my journey, Bergdorf Goodman catered to what I perceived as the older "rich" persons. The store was still under the supervision of Mr. Goodman. It was beautiful: mahogany walls in the dress department, always a huge fresh bouquet in a very large porcelain bowl, everything very sedate and expensive looking.

In those days, it seemed the chauffeured cars would pull up, one after the other, and dispense lovely, well-dressed women. I myself rarely came into the store before I began working there. It all seemed so bespoke and proper. One felt rather out of place just walking through. There were strict rules, including no returns in certain departments. The powers-that-be discouraged returns in general, and nobody protested.

The store wasn't in the least bit "trendy" and carried mostly American designers. When a new administration came in, they introduced an exciting world of European designers and opened the doors to a new, younger clientele. I have been through many administrations since then, and now everyone appears young to me (even the older "rich" persons). There continue to be changes in the store every day; I on the other hand have not changed my ways of picking out the clothes.

The way I pick and choose for an individual comes very easily to me. Once I know a client and have seen them in the dressing room, I never forget their size or look. Now I will try to explain in writing just how I work. It starts with a need; a client calls to say "I would like some new blouses." When it comes to my clients, I have learned to go halfway with what they think they "need." I could fill a whole book on people's desires.

To put together a wardrobe for a client, I start with the dressing room. I am very selective and I would say fussy about how I pull clothes for people. I gather outfits—suits, jackets, trousers, perhaps skirts, then blouses and shirts, depending on the season. Summer fare—shirts, lightweight trousers, pretty cotton dresses, long caftan dresses for fun summer evenings—is quick. Winter and fall, for me, are more interesting. Layering the fabrics is more challenging but, in the end, more satisfying.

No matter the season, however, I truly don't like separate pieces that don't go with other pieces of clothing. I often hear that they end up on a hanger, decorating the closet. Dressing well can be made very simple: a top and a bottom, and something newish to make the outfit exciting again for you. Buy good, wearable garments you can add to for longevity. Buy better. There is a certain security in the lasting.

When the room is set up for a client, it should look like a finely edited closet, grouped by category, and not a jumble of random pieces. With a beginning and an end, the rack tells a complete story. I am also in the dressing room to explain and show what can be. A great deal to selling is attitude and, yes, most importantly, knowledge. I have been at this for so long that most of the time I can see what fits the client—and it is not always the trendiest styles.

I take a long time with each individual client. I am not a multi-tasking person. I can handle only one thing at a time, otherwise I fall apart. I never rush them or get anxious over the time. I run out of patience when I haven't selected the right clothing (or the person is using me as a playmate as opposed to treating me with the dignity of a professional—but more on that later). It frustrates me beyond anything I could write about. I blame it all on myself. It's my fault that I haven't completed the job. As a young girl, I never handled defeat—let us call it—very well. At ninety-six, I still dwell on what I *haven't* accomplished. I am not a good loser.

Of course, no one person or thing is ever to blame. I am not a clothes magician. Let's return to the client who called for blouses. Sounds simple, doesn't it? Well, the season in which she called was pushing the '70s look—and yes, the blouses were oversized. Meanwhile this specific client is petite, which meant most of the season's blouses wouldn't be right. So when she came for her appointment, my job was to dissuade her from her original request. I pulled several tops, so she could see for herself. And she did. The client looked like a little girl swimming in her mother's clothes.

Knowing this would be the case, I had prepared some other pieces I thought would suit her—including a darling pleated shirtdress that fit her like a glove. When she twirled around, the starched belt elegantly framing her waist, I viewed the smile lit across her face. I love it when a client puts on a garment they love, particularly the last one she suspected she could wear, let alone buy.

*I don't go By The old adage—*
*"Clothes Make the Women"*
*a smile makes anyone look wonderful!*

# No One-Night Stands

WASTE IS ANATHEMA TO ME. I DON'T BELIEVE IN THROWING away food, relationships, or clothes. On my single bed, I cover myself up with the afghan my grandmother crocheted on her lap every Sunday, as her group of friends, "the girls," sipped coffee with whipped cream and nibbled hand-baked schnecken served on a silver platter with a doily. I marvel that after all of these years of use, it is in perfect condition.

When it comes to my wardrobe, I have never lived season to season. I have had some of my clothes for longer than most people have been alive. I give them a rest and then return to utilize them in a different way. Example, breaking up a suit, using the jacket as a separate and putting it together with a different skirt or trouser.

I do not sell clothing for a one-night stand. As I have said many a time and in many a way, longevity dressing is my favorite style. I liken clothes to paintings, which if of quality will increase in value and enjoyment with time (if cared for properly). I want the client to be able to wear a garment multiple times over many seasons, not once and done. You can change the accessories or context, but when you put it on, you should always feel stylish and right for the occasion.

One year I got my hands on an Issey Miyake dress. The pleated, navy dress looked different and marvelous on every body. I sold every single one of those dresses the store purchased. Meanwhile no one else touched the collection. Blessed with an eye, I am one step ahead, or I wouldn't be doing this. The dress went anywhere. Roll it up, pack it, and go—to a wedding, garden party, gallery opening. This is the kind of piece that once a year you take out and wear. It's a to-be-accessorized dress.

One may transform a garment through layering, but in the end there is hardly much need. People have short memories. Rarely do they remember the outfit you wore to a party.

In my book, the biggest compliment I receive is when someone says, "You sold me a dress ten years ago, and I still wear it."

While you can't always predict what will last and what won't, I suggest longevity a good thing to consider, and not only in your wardrobe. Think about it when you furnish your home, choose a job, and, most importantly, let people into your life.

*I am not a comedian by trade, however. I do like humor around me. Anything to distract from the real ME, who is trying to reinvent herself at every turn.*

# Happiness Is the Greatest Accessory

WHEN I WALK THROUGH THE STORE TO SEE NEW MERCHAN- dise, one floor at a time, I usually begin my adventure on the first floor. I am nothing if not methodical. This is the level that houses handbags, scarves, gloves, and hats. The first floor also boasts fine jewelry—a department that boggles the mind.

Cruising the extensive jewelry department, I am always bewildered to see the large cases with diamonds, rubies, and other costly pieces. I wonder, *Who stands at a counter in full view of Fifth Avenue and purchases those precious earrings, necklaces, and rings?* Someone must, as the huge department is long existing.

I don't pretend or even try to understand. I am not the department's typical customer. Not even when I was young, and well taken care of, did I crave expensive baubles. In marriage, we lived well, although Sonny didn't always agree with my wants, nor I with his. We often disagreed. My mother-in-law was satisfied with the extravagant jewelry of the postwar period like Marilyn Monroe wore in *Gentlemen Prefer Blondes*, but diamonds are not my thing. I love jewelry but of the sentimental variety, something with meaning from the giver.

# Another Good Accessory

I ALWAYS BRUSH MY CLOTHES. EVERYTHING IN MY CLOSET is very meticulous. I remember my mother using plastic tape to pick up lint, dust, hair, and whatever else clings to the cloth. While I keep a whole assortment of brushes in a basket in my closet so they are always at the ready, my favorite is Evercare's Magik Lint Brush (no, I am not a spokeswoman, at least not officially). When I take out a garment—particularly woolen jackets and sweaters that catch the lint, although I give everything, even silk, a once-over—I brush in one direction up the cloth and then down in the opposite motion. The brush has a "magic" cloth head that removes fuzz, hair, and other unwanted debris. You can use it on bedding and upholstery as well for a whole glorious day of dusting. Some people send their clothes out to the cleaners instead of giving them a good brush. I don't use cleaners that much. The harsh process takes everything off the fabric, which is not good. I have everything washed at home that I can, including woolen sweaters. However, brushing your clothes always and often will do wonders for their appearance. No suds involved.

# Indulge in Alterations

I'M A STICKLER FOR FIT. I AM VERY BIG ON THE RIGHT alterations, because they can make a tremendous difference in the clothes and body. Hemming sleeves or pant legs, taking in the waist, adjusting the darts, even moving the belt loops—these modifications, easily achieved by a skilled tailor, truly give the dress, jacket, or pant a very custom look. I do not, however, believe in alterations to the point of making a garment over. If the shoulders are too big on a blazer, return it to the rack immediately. That is quite a costly endeavor, and there are always more jackets in the sea. More often than not, though, I urge people to indulge themselves in tailoring. It is important to me and my taste level. Most, I must say, are more than willing to accept the service, and none are sorry when they do agree to a nip or tuck.

You need not shop on Fifth Avenue to find your own tailor. Many of the dry cleaners that everyone loves to frequent these days have someone who sews inside. You can start slow, the hem of a pant or sleeve that is a little too long. If you like the tailor's work, keep up the connection. There are some who value their relationship with their tailor over the one they have with their spouse!

# Taste Rules

TODAY WAS THE HEIGHT OF IT ALL. A T-SHIRT WITH A designer's name we all know attached to it arrived in stock, and when I saw the price tag I almost fell out of my chair—and for a woman of my years that could have proved fatal. Unfortunately, that was the only sane response to the request of nine hundred dollars for a cotton, round-neck, short-sleeve, uninteresting fabric garment. A thousand American dollars (when tax is factored in) for a T-shirt! How outrageous, decadent, and every expletive one could use to describe it. Even from my cloistered office, one wonders if there won't be an uprising in this country.

I am very conservative, in the original sense of "to conserve." I am known to tell my clients, "You are not here for me to get into your pocketbook and clean it." If I see a garment and I believe the price is too expensive—which in my book means the quality, artistry, or ingenuity is not reflected in the asking amount—I will not show it. Price does not rule my work: taste does.

Fortunately, I do not buy for the designer. In fact, I don't do "logo clothes." With all the logos on so much clothing, one has to wonder when wearing a designer's name on your chest became the in thing. It truly mystifies me.

I haven't sold a handbag—the ultimate in logo wear—in a very long time because I'm very particular about how the insides are made and how they close, and I don't like what I'm seeing. Instead, I go off in another direction. I'm here to find hidden gems. Not everything has to be top-end to look top-notch. A moderately priced pant can let a special top be the showstopper.

I wonder if the famous labels we all know won't become less important as they become prohibitively expensive. They who love clothing don't have to be consumed with a certain brand. Perhaps not being able to afford the hype of the rich and well-known is not a bad thing. It gives a chance to a lot of talent out there. I believe some good and new will be born out of this unreasonable time. That is the optimist in me. Say a quick hello since she doesn't come out often.

Back to the realist: I was browsing through the shoe department and picked up a pair of simple sneakers. I thought maybe I would indulge myself. Upon lifting one shoe to look at the price tag on the sole, I let out a gasp—two thousand dollars! That is something to put down on paper. No one would believe it if you told them.

A good rule of thumb is this: if you are ashamed to tell a friend the price of a garment or accessory you purchased, you probably paid too much. Don't assume that because something is expensive, it is of value. Look for unique, beautifully and carefully made items and happily pay their maker what they are worth.

# There Is Such a Thing as Too Casual

I'VE OBSERVED A TRANSFORMATION IN THOSE PASSING through the floors of the store. There is a whole new force getting off the elevators, wandering through the boutiques, and sitting in the bar in the restaurant on the seventh floor. The women are sporting athletic tights with their very costly handbags. In the restaurant, which has never been so filled, men in shorts expose their hairy legs. These groups are beyond casually dressed. Casual is putting it too lightly. Casual is too kind.

During the pandemic, when New York was under a lockdown, people got used to *not* going out or getting dressed at all. Fitness played a part. Everyone seemed to be toning up. Lululemon became an everyday thing. (Until very recently, I thought the brand's name was Lou Lou Lemon. My very young assistant informed me otherwise.) People became more relaxed in everyday life, and casual clothing found itself unconfined. You could go to work looking like you were about to jog through the park, and even to dinner!

Now we have reached the point where shorts are fine to go out in no matter the time of day! There are styles like the terrycloth trend, which I can't wrap my head around. In my world, terry cloth is a towel. Are they going to make towels into outerwear while we dry ourselves with Kleenex? Too silly.

The men have reached the bottom of the pole in dressing. The suit and necktie long disappeared, save for a blue moon. But when the workplace no longer required a dress coat, men went too casual, down to their shoes. What we used to call tennis shoes seem to be the footwear of choice for any and every occasion. Elders are taking a page from the younger person's book. They are also outfitting themselves in the tennis shoe, T-shirt, stretch pant, and, during colder months, puffer quilted coat. In one sentence, you have an entire wardrobe.

I cannot get used to it or hide my disdain. I like to look correct, which means everything color coordinated and some sort of pattern to my dressing. Accessories are most important to me: earrings, neck pieces, lapel pins—they are all part of each day's ensemble.

My head goes way back to how everyone who came into Bergdorf Goodman—and I mean *everyone*—once dressed. They adorned themselves in the newest outfits just to walk through the floors. You saw the most current clothes and accessories. It was a picture-perfect treat. There was never enough.

I'm from the "olden days," when we dressed in the morning for the day, then returned home in the late afternoon to refresh ourselves and change into what we thought was more appropriate for restaurant dining. Even if the reservation was at a steak house, we had an outfit for that. How nice it was to dress for the occasion. It made everything a bit special and helped an introvert to look forward to the night out.

We bought new clothes often, wore them, and bought more. It was an era where you liked being seen in something new. Our hair was done each week. Some had standing appointments at places like Elizabeth Arden. Local hair salons weren't yet in business, so you could spend many an hour just waiting to have your hair washed. It was a day's outing. Then you were always careful when you bathed or slept not to mess up the coif. Oh, what a different time.

That dress code doesn't exist anymore. Today, we all tend to dress in the morning—and are still in the same attire come evening. Maybe with the demise of fashion magazines, many persons have little direction. Most women are kind of "monkey see, monkey do." They need a plan visually spelled out loud and clear.

I am not suggesting we return to the old ways, where it took a whole day to get your hair done. But haven't we lost a small pleasure in everyday living and a different way to express ourselves that isn't verbal? I want to find an antidote to this new pandemic of casual dressing with a return to beautiful jackets, tailored trousers, and most of all, my favorite, dresses! Bring back fabrics, color, buttons, details! I know the world is not with me on this. No, no. After all, I'm an old person. This makes it so difficult for me to sell wardrobes, because it is not within me to offer up T-shirts as everyday wear. My thrust is to try to convince the client to be the first one on the block to look not drastically but a bit different. It gives them such a good feeling if they do.

I will say that for all my railing against the culture, I may be loosening up a bit myself. In all the years I have worked at the store I never came to work dressed as I recently did. I, who used to wear the look of the modern tailored workingwoman, arrived at Bergdorf Goodman in old black pull-on pants, a T-shirt for warmth, and a large turtleneck sweater. My excuse was that it was the weather. That day was snow-raining. On my feet I wore black sneakers as I don't own snow boots. True, I had a shell pin on my sweater and silver bracelets from my drawer filled with artifacts. Although I have become more casual myself, I will never give up accessorizing.

Recently I attended a holiday dinner at my neighbor's home, and the hostess's grandchildren, in their early thirties, all came dressed informally and yet beautifully. In my day, they wouldn't have dared arrive for dinner in anything other than a suit and tie. These fellows weren't in suits but instead wore mostly vintage sweaters and jackets from their grandfather's collection—and they looked terrific. They were casual but not sloppy.

Maybe my standards are slipping, but I don't think so. I believe the opposite of casual is care. You needn't wear a gown to show you put some thought into your appearance as a gesture of respect to your hosts or others in your presence. Grandad's canary-yellow cable-knit under a tweed jacket adds just as much to the loveliness of the event.

# Break Away from the Herd

TOO MUCH OF FASHION THESE DAYS SUFFERS FROM THE herd mentality. January is with us, and though not one snowflake have I seen, everyone is in their puffer coats. Never mind that the temperature is in the fifties. Aren't we a silly go-by-the-fashion-rules society? Not me, I won't, shan't, can't!

I suspect there is a certain security attached to being one of the gang, but buying the same expected look over and over is not what I do. My taste is eclectic in all things—from my style of decor to my clientele to the company I keep. I like things that are offbeat, different, and I don't mean peculiar. Eclecticism presents a challenge that keeps me going, alert, and current.

Not one of my clients is cloned. No two persons are alike, so why would they dress alike? It simply doesn't make sense. Each and every one is entitled to their own taste and opinion. That is chapter and verse in my bible. I encourage it by seeking out the new and adventurous for all my clients. I built a reputation on diversification.

Crafting a wardrobe is a game with me, much like how I cook these days. For example, today I found a corned beef, to which I added some sauerkraut and herbs, then a pineapple to finish. Truly an add-on game and like the way I sell clothes—a piece here, another there, all over the place, until it's a complete dish.

Recently, I discovered a hand-quilted jacket with a flower motif reminiscent of a bedspread and a sheer, short-sleeved blouse with graphic embroidery by a small downtown designer who had initially made a name for herself with her menswear. I consider her quilted coat quite an upgrade from the dime-a-dozen Chanel jacket. These are very special things, but not everyone wants to be special.

I am known to find the one outfit that would be difficult, if not impossible, to locate elsewhere. Designers that other people pass on because their eye takes them to the ordinary, I am drawn to. When I present the unexpected to a client, an item they never experienced let alone imagined themselves wearing, they invariably turn to me after taking it in for a moment and ask the age-old question: "What do you think?"

"It isn't what I think," I say. "It is: 'How do you feel?'"

As much as I push my clients to take risks, I don't want them to defer to my taste. I will not be there when they are wearing the clothes. My hope is they make the delightful discovery that they look wonderful in something they would have never picked off the rack.

Perhaps that's the reason I get truly exasperated with a client when they absolutely refuse to try on anything new or different. "Why are you here if you didn't hope for any type of change?" I ask. In response, some disappear. More often, however, they put a toe in the water and enjoy the thrill of the unexpected. They come in sad and walk out very happy. That is the power of metamorphosis.

Although the familiar is comforting, no matter how much we wish for it, nothing stays the same: not the names of designer labels, the power dynamic with children, the partners in our beds, the reason we get up in the morning.

It is boring to follow the trends and be contented with mimicry. Open your mind to new possibilities.

*Long on the tongue, I am not out to hurt anyone. I just tell them what I think!*

# The Perils of Shopping in a Group

TODAY, THERE WAS A BARRAGE OF FOUR PEOPLE WHO ALL turned up at the office within the same hour. This upsets me to no end because I am meticulous when it comes to my calendar. I carefully block my time so that I am never pulled in more than one direction. One person at a time—this person receiving my undivided attention—has always been my way of working. There is a reason it is called "personal shopping." While most private shoppers go from telephone to telephone or dressing room to dressing room, for me, it truly is a one-on-one activity. Intimacy reaps rewards. Once I am in a room with someone, I don't leave them for anyone else. I can't be distracted from them. I am completely immersed in their brain.

Ironically, new clients almost always arrive for their first appointment with an entourage. *Ammunition*, I like to call the attending crowd. Whether it's a friend, mother, daughter—even a child—I can say no one comes in on their own. As I lead the troop through the store, I feel like the Tour Guide of Bergdorf Goodman.

I have always found doing what I do in a group very unsuccessful as everyone has different thoughts as well as tastes. It's part of why I believe being sequestered in a hidden corner of the third floor is a very big plus. Seclusion is one of the hallmarks of my operation. It takes courage to try new things and face new situations. However, I find people are much more willing to take risks if they don't have an audience around.

If you feel unsure of your taste, do take one trusted friend shopping with you. But don't ask for help from anyone for whom jealousy is a factor. Choose an unbiased friend who is reasonable and will tell you the truth. The hardest part of that assignment is finding such a friend!

# We All Need a Reason to Leave the House

THE ADVENT OF THE COMPUTER AND SCROLLING ONLINE means so much more "store" at your fingertips. One can sit at home, pull up to the computer, and have an entire department to oneself. You don't even need a computer anymore as smartphones seem to offer the same experience.

I'm reminded of how everyone is stuck on computer shopping each time I pass the store's delivery room in the morning. There I find towers of corrugated brown boxes: returned online orders! Do we realize that the new zillionaires might just be the persons in the brown box business? The towering cardboard is proof of impulsive and dissatisfied customers scarily powered by the speed of technology. My greatest fear is this kind of boredom, which creates a hunger nothing can satisfy. I'm often critical of excess. When I was a teenager my mother and father accused me of being "a communist with a loaf of bread under each arm." Perhaps let's just say I'm a socialist?

I am certainly for the worker, and those of us who stand here with real feet and real eyes to see are privy to the destruction of the unfeeling and uncaring computer. The problem is that online sales literally take away merchandise from the brick-and-mortar (or, in the case of Bergdorf Goodman, South Dover white marble) store. They're not *two* stores, and yet we're competing with ourselves. My clients become agitated that those who order online are first to get information and their deliveries—and if they don't, I agitate for them. The physical has become secondary.

This is a very involved and difficult-to-fix issue about the true definition of progress. Admittedly, I am a living antique. There are times I sort of wish I were like the rest of the world and put my head and hands to the computer or cell phone. However, the reality is I do not wish to be like the rest of the world. Sharing the same habits with everyone else bothers me. My feeling has always to be a bit different. One learns so much that way. Going through the back door to reach what you are searching for makes every day a new experience.

I don't care for any kind of shopping online, including shopping for groceries. Unlike most people, I like grocery shopping. I have truly enjoyed trips to the grocer since childhood, when it was always a very special time together with Mother. I treat the market like most persons treat Bergdorf Goodman. The bread displays, cheeses from all over the world mounded up, colorful spices: it's all wonderful, but there is nothing more intriguing to me than the produce department. I love finding the biggest, greenest artichoke or lettuce in a variety I've never seen before. Fresh produce is as beautiful to me as any flower arrangement. I've been known to become friendly and acknowledge the men mounding, sorting, and unpacking the produce. They can always dig in and hand me the freshest, long-lasting vegetable. I make friends with important people.

I am not above plunging my own hands into the bin, touching nearly every potato before putting one into a bag. I might turn every head of a lettuce over before choosing one or leaving it altogether to search for a different kind. I am not a grocer's delight or idea of a great patron, but I'm used to myself. I am meticulous not only with vegetables but also with my kitchen cabinets, the clothes in my closet, the pieces I pick out for my clients—actually, my entire life.

Although I don't get around nearly as well as I used to, I still relish my visit to the grocery store, where I go each weekend with a list of what I need and my upstairs neighbor, who graciously carries my load home, one bag on each shoulder. I enjoy roaming the aisles, discovering different brands and ingredients I have never and might never buy or cook with. The eye experience is so much more interesting and appealing in real life than on a screen.

Nothing can replace going to a store, whether it's for a loaf of raisin bread, a silk blouse, or a birthday gift. Isn't giving usually because one wants to find something that suits the recipient, whether serious, joyful, or quirky, but done with thought? How can that be achieved by turning on the computer, scanning sites, and—pop—sending, without even seeing the real thing? That just does not register with me. Isn't it almost a rather

## NO ONE HAS SEEN IT ALL

unfeeling way of purchasing something for a person you care for? Not to mention the dreaded brown box that has become the gift packaging of the modern day. Gone are beautiful papers, exquisite bows, handprinted cards.

Computer buying is so insular and lacks the excitement of getting out in the retail world. Being able to see the colors with your own eyes, feel the fabrics in your hand, and try the silhouette on your figure is worth more than any computer. How about also seeing other live humans around you and perhaps talking to one or two?

From living so long, I know this online shopping trend will wear itself out and something new will appear on the horizon. I just don't have the privilege of time to see what it will be. However, I recommend to anyone who will listen, pick your head up from the screen and get out into the world. Walk the store's floor, touch the dress or jacket you think you like, locate personnel who can help you. Let's return to an existence filled with some sort of interaction. We all need to dress and leave our homes; make shopping a destination.

*Even tho' my hearing is not what it once was (I never sorted out the hearing situation!) I am still a listener. It is a matter of attitude not biology!*

ON DRESSING

# Wearing the Newest Is Not What It Once Was

I AM A WOMAN WHO SINCE AS LONG AS I CAN REMEMBER has always loved, *loved* clothes. Every new season I would relish something new and just have to add it to my wardrobe. The theater, opera, ballet, new luxurious restaurants—all of these required new seasonal outfits.

In my married life we dressed up every Saturday night, whether we were headed out to a supper club or nightclub. Meeting at the newest restaurants, we often were as many as five couples—ten of us! My father-in-law, friendly with the gambling kinds, always got the best table at Danny's Hideaway and the steak houses. Everyone wore their very best for dinner and then dancing at the Copacabana or listening to music at late, late clubs in the Village where you entered after midnight. We went all over the city and even across the river to New Jersey, where Ben Marden's Riviera always had the best and current stars, such as Lena Horne or Dean Martin.

Social life in New York City during those postwar years was very exciting and sometimes overwhelming. It seemed everyone was looking to start over, find a new way. Frankly, it frightened me. I knew nothing about gambling, nightclubs, flashy jewelry, and high dressing. My lifestyle at "home" in Chicago was elegant, good food and pretty clothes. But it was filled with families, who congregated for dinner parties, not high livers running around town with large rolls of cash in their pockets.

Almost as soon as I arrived in New York City, all I wanted to do was go back to Chicago. Change has never been my friend. I had a very difficult time communicating in the restaurants, nightclubs, and after-hours joints my husband and his father took me to. I was surrounded by hard men, and I had absolutely nothing in common with any of them. Maybe that's a reason films like *The Godfather* are not interesting to me. I often wonder, Does any of this lively underworld of eating, drinking, and dancing still exist? I am quite sure it does. Today, I do believe I could handle it and perhaps understand some of it. I'll never know since I am not going to attempt to find out.

I purchase so very few clothes today. I've definitely lost the zest for always appearing in the newest. In the morning, I wander into my closets, pulling out this pair of trousers or that jacket—mixing and matching between the old and very old. At this age, my former excitement over dressing seems to have left me. I always want to look presentable and put together, down to the piece of jewelry on my lapel. But—and it is a large *but*—the need for fresh pieces is gone. Gone. Did it become too easy for me? The shoemaker's wife syndrome? Now it's almost awaken, rise, dress, be gone. I wish this had come earlier in my life. Maybe it's the security I have at last unearthed.

ON DRESSING

After a lifetime of accumulating, it is normal that I would be sated with my wardrobe. However, I do believe that I am also in vogue. Wearing the very latest has become so unimportant in today's fashion world. More and more are digging into their closets, finding treasures they are happy to wear again. What I have been doing for years has become a fad. How many times have I heard, "Where did you get that?" from young people, admiring the old clothes I wear to work?

Not only have I truly lost interest in buying new clothes, I also don't feel much in how others dress. I start at the top—what's going on in the mind—and work my way down. To me, a person's intellectual state is much more important than their trousers. I don't mean it in a snobbish way. Rather, how do you approach life? Do you learn a little bit each day or truly take in the world around you with curiosity? That's my favorite style.

*There is nothing new constantly going through my mind. Sometimes this can be helpful. Other times it can be very detrimental. It may, and can hold you back from moving forward. Extremely complex!*

# ON MANNERS

# Treat Others as You Wish to Be Treated

WHEN A NEW CLIENT, WHO HAD ARRIVED FIRST THING IN THE morning, was still trying on clothes at the end of the day, I began to lose patience—something I was not born with a lot of. Even bridal shopping and the most complex fittings typically don't last more than several hours. But it wasn't the length of time this woman was taking that bothered me. As I've said, I don't like to rush or push when it comes to the intimacy of my work.

It has been my experience that some women enter a fantasy in the dressing room. Glued to their mirror image, they get farther from reality with every piece of the many clothes they try. This becomes a long, long, tiring event for me. I have termed it "playtime."

I left the client above alone in the fitting room to take a break at my desk, where I used my trusty legal pad to exorcise some of these negative thoughts. Returning to the dressing room, however, I found the woman trying on the same clothes we started with in the morning! Now it was more evident to me than ever that this had become a game, and an all-day one. When she handed me the discarded items to hang up, I wondered how people like this were brought up.

Today, manners have some sort of an old-fashioned connotation. However, I think that's a mistake. What does it express when you hold a door open for someone exiting or say "please" when making a request? It doesn't mean you come from a time when people still got around town in a horse and buggy. No, it says that you recognize that another human being stands there, in flesh and blood, right in front of you—and that you care. Today there is no longer any protocol. Anywhere. People wear sweatpants to work because their workplace is on their couch! Never mind holding a door open; there's nobody to enter it. Everyone seems to be marching to their own drummer. I worry it's going to do us in.

I grew up in an age when manners were a huge part of one's upbringing. Consequently, they are instinctive to me. I don't have to think about putting my napkin on my lap before eating or standing whenever someone enters a room, no matter how young they are or how old I am. I can tell you that the minute someone comes in my office—and that's an awful lot of people, some just to look and see if I'm still here—I get on my feet immediately. It's a welcome, a sign of appreciation, and an acknowledgment all rolled into one.

I'm always so pleased (and, frankly, shocked) when someone extends a hand or rises from their chair to greet an elder. Old-fashioned for sure, but there is a graciousness attached. I'm sad to see it all disappear in the rush to go nowhere.

With the new client still playing dress-up in the changing room, my humor and glad-to-see-you attitude is long gone. I am, however, not allowed to let her see me lose my patience. My good manners will not allow me. I try to run this office as if it were my own house, that is, with decorum. My thoughts go way back to the days when I was on the other side of the retail equation and how I purchased clothes. I wouldn't treat anyone differently than how I would wish to be treated.

Manners can give you such a big leg up. They are very charming and don't cost anything. Nothing. Nada.

*Children are brought up so casually today. No monograms. Their way of dressing alone tells the story!*

# Put Down the Cell Phone

I AM THE FIRST ONE TO ADMIT I PICK UP THE PHONE FOR companionship. Whereas I used to feel it was intrusive, I now wait for the welcoming ring and communication at the other end. I am not, however, talking about the cell phone. That is not a mode of communication; it is an addiction.

Admittedly, I use none of the world's new contraptions, mobile phone or computer. I recognize that young persons reading this will be mystified by the description "new" when talking about these things that for them are as essential as air and water. Maybe they will feel similarly about flying cars, talking dogs, or whatever is coming down the pike.

Back to the present: I have noticed that the cell phone does not seem to leave its owner's hand. I remember the days when it was still a nonentity, and now everyone's head and ears are stuck to them. It has become a fifth limb. I have seen people who upon believing they have misplaced their phone become as hysterical as if they had lost an engagement ring or small child. How about when you are conversing with someone, or at least trying to, and they constantly glance at the cell phone in their clutch? It reminds me of the Manhattan cocktail parties of my youth, where you could spot a social climber by how their eyes darted around the room while talking.

There is one good thing about these contraptions: they are filled with information. All in one, this instrument holds multitudes. One doesn't need a dictionary, atlas, or any other book of knowledge. It is all there in a small handheld device! A miracle, yet a very invasive business.

Just as I give my clients my undivided attention, so I request theirs in return. The longstanding ones know better than to pick up their cell phones during a fitting. I don't scold or scowl. Instead, I simply raise an eyebrow and remark, "Must you?" They rarely pick up the phone after that.

From a ninety-six-year-old: my future does not have much longevity, but as long as I inhabit this planet I wish for some togetherness! A little eye contact would be a good start.

*I am not a canceller. I do not believe in cancelling. I suffer from the dread syndrome, so no matter what the occasion or task, I like to get on with it and get it over.*

# Late Is Not Fashionable

I AM ALWAYS EARLY. ALWAYS. LAST NIGHT, I SAT IN MY apartment for over forty minutes, completely ready, purse in hand, waiting for my dinner date to call up from the lobby. He was not late; it was I who was early. Forty minutes early. I try to be late, but I just can't. It's bred in me somehow. I've had to walk around many a block in my time.

Although I believe that being chronically late is, simply, bad manners, I am not in the majority. I don't know whether those who are always "on their way" think they are being fashionable, because that's not how I operate. When it comes to my business, I demand on-time behavior. If you've been held up by traffic or other unforeseen events, a notice by call, email, or text to my office is appreciated. You don't even need a quarter anymore to telephone, so there really is no excuse. Communication, however, goes only so far in my book. I see only one person at a time, so if someone else has arrived before you due to your lateness, I am on to the next and it's your hard luck. I don't have to punish the overly tardy; they punish themselves.

I've heard the excuse that those who are always keeping others waiting don't mean to be rude. They are just bad with time. Their heads are in the clouds. Unencumbered by the burden of a clock or watch, they are spirited away by whatever or whoever crosses their path.

Well, I'm not moved by those explanations. I think more should care about being on time than do presently. I believe some are late in order to make themselves seem more important. They are searching for a recognition of sorts.

It happened the other day. The occasion was my birthday, not an event I am too eager to mark as I've never been good with numbers and mine are getting pretty high up there! However, a group of friends insisted we go out for lunch to celebrate. As one might imagine, most everyone in my set is punctual. There is one exception, and, like clockwork, she came late—so late, she missed the meal altogether. She arrived as we were finishing dessert, but we expected as much, so it was nothing out of the ordinary. We all just looked at one another and laughed.

Save your grand entrances for the stage and just be on time. You will make a much larger and happier impression.

# Handwritten Notes Never Go Out of Style

NO ONE SEEMS TO PICK UP A PEN ANYMORE. TODAY, ONE gets a congratulatory email. Consequently, the news, thank-yous, happy birthdays, whatevers—all are communicated digitally. Not terribly personal, I would say.

For me, feelings come through the pen. I treasure my correspondences with family, friends, designers, creative humans, and clients (who are also, often, friends in kind). Many are saved in thick bundles kept together with rubber bands or ribbon. How could I part with a hand-drawn card from the genius Maira Kalman, a thank-you from one of my oldest clients for her daughter's marathon wedding gown fitting, or a letter from Japan from a young reader of my memoir in translation? My mother was a note writer par excellence. Dashed off in black ink on her personal stationery, they mimicked her famous wit.

It takes but a few minutes to write a note, and there is an intimacy to even the hastiest handwritten communication that can never be achieved in the lengthiest of emails. Plus, good stationery is a joy to shop for and purchase. The cards I keep in the office have my likeness, scribbled a long time ago by William Ivey Long, a talented costume designer who could moonlight as a maker of Christmas cards. (I keep a stack from our decades-long friendship.) I had William's doodle printed on cards, and underneath it is written "from the desk of Betty Halbreich." If you pick up the writing habit, as I hope you will, indulge in personal note cards created just for you.

# Clean Plate Club

DECEMBER 26: THE THANK-YOU NOTES ARE WRITTEN AND put in envelopes to be mailed; a chicken is in the skillet cooking for tonight's supper; the plants are watered, and new water poured into the flower arrangements. And this was all done on a beautiful Sunday afternoon.

Being an overly orderly person, I am always striving for a clean plate. I try to cross off everything on my to-do list, practically and emotionally. A lot on my plate tends to undo me. Even phone messages that have piled up send me to the moon. Consequently, my business has always run in a very mannerly way.

Today no one knows what that means. The pandemic took whatever decorum was hanging on by its fingernails and pushed it to its doom. I do find that in this new business world we are living in, persons are very slow to communicate, if you can get hold of them at all. You can make a call with a question that, not too long ago, you would expect a quick reply to. Now you call again, twice—each time the phone going directly to an answering service—send an email, and often still do not get an answer. Nothing. It is embarrassing to have to keep at it. I feel like a nuisance repeating the calls, so I often just turn the page. Returning messages has been replaced by a great deal of silence. It leaves me with much angst.

Whether etiquette, in any form, will return remains to be seen. Unsure about the future, people are paralyzed when it comes to making plans or making up their minds. No one can be more uncertain about what tomorrow will bring than me! I am ninety-six, after all. Yet to leave someone hanging without resolution—good, bad, or indifferent—is frustrating. Not to mention a difficult way to make a buck.

Hanging on a very short fuse, I want everything done, completed immediately. No wait time. This has always been my temperament ever since I was old enough to have memories, and with age it grows more intense. I'm so aware of every moment of this need to accomplish, but I find little to no control to temper the instinct. So I suffer.

In life, there is a beginning but also an ending. I never leave calls unanswered, even difficult ones. For when the problem is solved and over, I offer up thanks, a bit superstitious. The old adage "clean your plate" has always worked for me, and I am not about to change. It isn't just a psychological relief. Thanks in part to my near half century of prompt rejoinders, when I reach out to well-known design houses, stylists, and writers, I hear back quickly. This is so rewarding, honest, and how the world should be run.

This is all a little easier for me since I don't use email, which I understand from hearsay only proliferates the more you reply. Still, I recommend turning Friday into clean-the-desk day as it always has been for me. Get everything in order for the following week, returning messages and finishing up left-behind tasks. This way you can put your head to rest and be revitalized for the coming week.

> I have worked hard all these years because I wanted to. I truly do not know any other way to function.

# The Telephone Line Goes Both Ways

I PICK UP THE PHONE FOR COMPANIONSHIP. IT DOES KEEP ringing. My second call today was from a delightful person who makes beautiful jewelry, although when we first met, she was a pastry chef. We talked about her son's wedding, grocery shopping, and her garden, where she keeps a pot of lilies of the valley and thinks of me as each sprig comes up. Not one word about business. Delightful.

Some others call most every day to tell me their problems. I am a very good listener because my attitude is "But for the grace of God go I." It is quite easy for me to put myself in other's shoes; indeed, I have often walked in those selfsame shoes!

My conversational companions are of all ages. Only one is my age, which makes sense. How many live so long? There aren't many old ladies so fortunate as to be asked to listen, let alone out to dinner, events, even lunch—all on a regular basis. At any age, this is a miracle. Sunday is the day I play catch-up on the phone. I have never liked to do it from the office as it interferes with business. At home, it is a social call, or, at least, it should be.

On one such Sunday in 2021, I reached out to the cowriter of my first book. Although it had been more than twenty-five years since we worked together, I've always been fond of her and her very professional ways. Our book continued to sell until rather recently when the publisher decided to stop printing copies. I know because I continued to receive the royalty checks. That wasn't my motivation for reaching out to my writer. Rather it was her location: Boulder, Colorado. Horrible wildfires had just erupted and were burning down hundreds of homes. I got her on the phone, and what a rewarding call it was. She was so delighted to hear from me, and I to learn she and her family were safe from the fire. I felt good; she felt good—a blessing just a phone call away.

We must reach out more to those we think of and not wait for as extreme an instance as a raging wildfire. For someone to know you are thinking of them is a very rewarding gift with little in the way of cost or time.

# ON KEEPING HOUSE

# Mopping Is Good Therapy

TODAY I FOUND IT DIFFICULT TO PUT EVEN SIMPLE THOUGHTS together. Not even the pen, off which words usually fly, conjured anything better than many variations on a single theme: depression.

If one has never experienced these dark feelings, they can be very difficult to understand. I have endured them for most of my life. At certain times of the year—like the holidays, which continue to arrive no matter how long I live—depression easily creeps up in the wee hours of the night or suddenly at work. It knows no bounds.

My instinct tells me that I inherited this cloud that hangs above my head. The stormy weather traveled from my grandmother to my mother and finally found its way into my being. I can't ask them, although I am confident they would agree.

The feelings become second nature, so much so you may even get used to them. Or you can try to wish them away. I suggest neither methodology. As I do not want depression to become my middle name, I catch it in a hurry and quickly throw it to the winds. I have found picking up the yellow pad and writing helps a great deal, but it doesn't rid me of the dark feelings.

Instead, it brings them to the surface. When I want to simply shrug them off, which I do often, I succeed in that endeavor by making what I call "busywork."

I feel fortunate I can always make busywork in my apartment of—dare I say it—seventy years. (Contemplating that number alone is enough to send one out the window.) In my classic eight-room prewar apartment, there is always a closet, refrigerator, even the pots and pans department to tackle. Washing up can be a full-time job.

The kitchen, a store in itself, can take many days. The often-complimented wallpaper is wipeable, so that the orange-red poppies and green leaves look as fresh as they did when I purchased it nearly fifty years ago. I don't know if they even make washable wallpaper anymore. It's very clever but takes work.

I clean the kitchen in stages. However, my fridge must be very tidy at all times. Leftovers are carefully wrapped and not pushed to the back. Too much gets lost on the back of shelves. We are all guilty of left-behind leftovers, so many secret bottles, containers, and dishes. To be perfectly sure your food is updated in the refrigerator, everything—*everything*—should be removed periodically and thrown away.

Isn't it a phenomenon how very overpacked one's freezer can become? With me being a neatnik, mine is stacked properly. All in its right place. Cleaning out the refrigerator is a throwback to when I was a child. I loved Thursdays, when the maids were on their day off. Mother and I would cook dinner or order in Chinese—the only takeout I have ever enjoyed. We two would have an evening of putting the refrigerator to rights. This was after trips to the delicatessen with my father, who would take me on special Sundays to "buy out" the place. Or so I believed, because we came home with all sorts of food, and my mother would scream at him, "What are we going to do with it!"

"I don't care," he exclaimed. "If you don't like it, throw it away!"

That infuriated Mother even more.

I must admit that with my own freezer inventory, sometimes I do forget to label the container and, later, when removed, it becomes mystery food. Frequently, I find something delicious from long ago.

In the pantry I have a collection of silver that would make the British monarchy blush. Now that I no longer entertain, which was the raison d'être of my old life, many of the filigreed serving spoons, scimitar-like cake knives, and flatware so heavy one gets a workout in taking a forkful remain nestled in special silver bags cloistered in the upper shelves or corner drawers of my pantry. However, that does not mean there is no polishing to be done. The large silver tray atop a wheeling luggage cart is as spotless as it was the days I rolled it, laden with canapes, into the living room where guests sipped cocktails before dinner. I have a collection of silver frames all filled with photos. They can take a day of polishing to keep them looking their silver selves. The silver decanters, long drained of their whiskey and scotch, still sit on the bar, and my mother's lavish candelabra, although deprived of candles, has pride of place on the gleaming mahogany dining room table. Tarnish is intolerable on such treasures.

Constructive time relieves the boredom. This is a truth I've known since I was a young and only child, growing up in an apartment alone with household maids and little family around. With my dollhouse to keep me company, when I grew tired of arranging and rearranging its rooms, I would always tend to my dresser drawers and closets. These habits have taken me through childhood, adolescence, and adulthood.

Believe me, there is always something to do in daily living, things people never even think of doing, like turning your mattress over or pushing the furniture out of its nesting place and vacuuming underneath. If rugs are your choice, do vacuum them and give them a rotation or turn them on the other side!

A young friend extolled the virtues of her robotic vacuum during one of our phone chats. "I love it so much," she swooned. "I just wish it would also mop."

"Oh, no, no!" I cried. "Don't let go of that. Mopping is good therapy."

Most people I know loathe cleaning and straightening. A dear, beautiful, clever friend in the theatrical business found herself gone lost when her longtime housekeeper moved out of state. She did not have a clue as to how to turn on the washing machine, and to add to that, the dishwasher! My advice: Have the housekeeper walk you through their routine and video it using your cell phone (in this case, I approve of the device). How about they teach you how to boil water while you are at it?

You who maybe will read this long love letter will probably tire of my cleaning escapades. But here I go anyway.

It cheers me up; I find it rewarding. After a leak from an upstairs apartment meant a messy construction job in mine, the super sent in professional cleaners to finish the job. I didn't need that. They don't clean as well as I do, because they do it for a living; I for my sanity.

Keep brushing, sweeping, washing, and don't dare look at your hands or nails. When patience is difficult or days alone are too long, I am blessed with skill in the art of diversion. I know how to find solace in ironing the perfect pleat and corner on a napkin.

The gratification of an immaculate closet or ironed sheets may seem like a silly gratification; however, housework uses energy when we can't put it out in the real world. At ninety-six, I thank the dear Lord I am still equipped to push a broom. I run from room to room dusting, and because my preference is for fresh air over air-conditioning, soot, that occupational hazard of New York City living, is ever present. I do up the windowsills and around the windows. I like to do the inside of windows as well.

It is quite a marathon in this eight-room apartment. *Another cleanup day at the mansion*, I say.

Remove artifacts on a table or desk and bring out ye olde furniture polish to give life to hidden surfaces. In my case, this is no easy feat. The desks—which I never use, preferring to write in the den, sitting by the window—are bric-a-bracked to the hilt. The one in the living room is a real set piece, serving as a resting place for my collection of snuffboxes. I don't know when or why I began acquiring the little enameled pieces (that might go for all my collections, of which I have many). Perhaps I became enchanted with the two pigeons kissing atop one of the little boxes or the phrase "You are witty and pretty" written on another one spoke to me. They certainly serve no purpose other than to delight the eye, a metaphor I do not wish to contemplate!

The above are just a few of the things I have learned to keep busy and in action. They're good not only for the body but also the brain. Whether you pick up a book, do your hair, clean out a kitchen drawer—it all helps when you find yourself on the loneliness spectrum. Activity washes sad thoughts away, even if only for a short time. There is always something we can do to distract from the bad. I have succeeded in it many times over the years. Admittedly, sometimes not too easily. As long as one recognizes the symptoms of sadness, busywork can ward them off.

In the dark hours of the night, I am less controlled. As with many persons, "bad stuff" creeps into my half-asleep mind, such as the past, which I like to put far away. I should write after midnight. Putting thoughts down on the legal pad is, alas, another cleaning of sorts. Maybe I will try. Although as a child I was never allowed to put the light on or put a foot out of the bed until the allotted hour.

I believe structure is how we burrow out of the bad things. Today I batted away a bit of gloom when I found some lentils in the cupboard and used them to make an improvised salad. Onward now to straighten a closet, and hopefully tomorrow will bring a smile to a worn face.

Organizing your external world helps to organize your internal one as well. Tidying, cleaning, call it what you will, is a settling, regulating, and pleasurable exercise. It is a true catharsis, going through one's life, old or new.

*It is human Nature to Become Bored at Times— EVEN tho' There might Be Ecommic depressions, pandemics, and EVEN WARS!*

# Books Are the Best Decor

I LOVE TO BE SURROUNDED WITH BOOKS. IN MY OFFICE, there are many more books than items of clothing. Coffee table tomes by friends, such as the photographer Ruven Afanador or illustrator Maira Kalman, rise in weighty pyramids on my desk. Memoirs, novels, and how-tos from clients and friends line the base of my window. At home, my bookshelves are at capacity. Whereas I'm known to purge bags of designer garments with each season, I'm loath to dispose of or even give away any of my books. They are my absolute favorite decor. They warm a room, cozy it up. If I were younger and starting over again, the first thing I would do is put in new, additional bookshelves in my den at home. Nonetheless, I can always find space for a book on the table next to my bed. For me there is nothing more comforting than climbing into bed at a reasonable hour, pitching up three pillows, and having a good read. I keep some fresh flowers in a vase next to the bed, and in the background a myriad of family photos in their nostalgic silver frames. That's all I require at day's end.

# Give Away Your Things Before You're Dead

I OPEN THE CUPBOARDS IN THE KITCHEN PANTRY—QUIETLY digging into my past life—and admire a tray made from a hand-embroidered linen preserved under glass. The little roses of French knots are now faded as they were sewn by my grandmother the year I was born. I know because she stitched her initials, *JDR*, and the date, *November 1927*.

I am, of course, spending a Sunday organizing the kitchen cabinets. I have neatened, arranged, rearranged, folded, and looked through drawers so that there truly isn't anything left untouched. Being an overly orderly person, I am kind of running out of tidying up. (It's too bad I can't get a ladder and paintbrush and do the apartment walls. That would be the day. What a way to depart!) Each time I tackle a shelf or drawer, the same thought goes through my mind: *When I'm gone, left this planet, I want my children, or whoever is going through my possessions, at least to see order.*

Surveying my apartment these days, I see mountains of possessions of a long lifetime. In the strata of stuff, a history. Among the china, silver, bric-a-brac, books, pictures, silver sewing pieces, collections of whatever made me whole at the time, there is evidence of a younger me who always wanted more. And now? I must care for and eventually dispense them. Otherwise I worry what my children will have to undertake when I am gone. I imagine those huge dump trucks I see roaming the neighborhood: *We Take Junk*. They pull up to the front door and all you have to do is dump! What a pity, because from my long experience, what comes around goes around. One can't hold one's breath for that time, however.

Are my grandchildren ready and waiting for a Royal Crown Derby dinner service for twenty-four that sits on the top shelf of my kitchen's old-fashioned pantry? Four shelves of the cupboards that run to the ceilings hold china cups and saucers, dinner plates, dessert sets, tea sets, collectibles—salt and pepper sets, even a powdered sugar shaker! To the right, there are soufflé pots in which I baked little chocolate soufflés long ago. Underneath are kidney-shaped plates I purchased on a trip in Italy and used to serve salad. Decorated delicately with blue flowers and gold accents, they look as if someone had folded over a corner of the plate. I simply adore them, just as I do the goblets with bunches of grapes cut from their milk glass. On and on. I have my grandmother's hors d'oeuvre plates from Hungary and my mother's majolica, a style of tin-glazed pottery that mimicks the shapes of vegetables or fruits, like cabbage leaves or scooped-out melon halves, in which you can serve the real thing. I treasure my mother's corn plates and platter, from which I used to dish out sweet summer corn from the South Fork.

NO ONE HAS SEEN IT ALL

It's a wonder these old shelves can stand up against the weight of this haul, which includes pewter molds we used for cranberry jelly or put in the freezer filled with different ice cream flavors for dinner parties. The smaller ones held chicken liver pâté decorated with sliced olives (green with pimento stuffing!).

The last shelves, housing silverware, have not been mentioned. In the days when I was married, silver pieces were a huge part of wedding gifts. Not today. No one for starters wants to care for and polish it. When I came to New York, we first moved into a small apartment where my silver collection took up much room. That soon changed when a woman working for me relieved me of my burden by taking many pieces into her possession. She removed them slowly, piece by piece, but it was a quick lesson for a newlywed girl of twenty when I discovered them gone. I still own a goodly amount today—it's wrapped in special tissue paper and bags with some tarnish-proof strips. I rarely visit or polish the majority of my collection. It's too much upkeep, and in no time tarnished again.

More than I can dig into, it is all so beautiful and so of the past. My huge selection of cookbooks—some of which I have given to the handsome, lovely man who runs our restaurants at the store—brings back memories of lush dinner parties that took many weeks of planning. I read the cookbooks I collected like one reads a novel. After settling on a menu, I'd set out on the familiar route to our local grocer, butcher, and other purveyors—all knew our cook, Frieda, and me quite well.

ON KEEPING HOUSE

During my married life, there was truly no reason to go shopping outside our Upper East Side neighborhood. My butcher shop was run by three generations of the same family. The greengrocer—who would come out of the store to say hello when I walked by—allowed you to "finger" the fruits and vegetables. The dry cleaner, the tallest man, would have something cleaned and pressed for you the same day. There were myriad local stores: Flora Mir sold the best licorice on the corner of Madison Avenue. William Greenberg's first bakery appeared next to the grocer and brought the smells of schnecken and coffee cake. His bakery is now an institution, but in those early days Mr. Greenberg could be found in the window decorating birthday cakes and many-tiered wedding cakes.

It wasn't only food we shopped for. If you turned the block, you ran into a small shoe repair store where a lovely Italian man and his wife worked long hours making your beaten-up shoes good as new. The flower shop across the street sold the first lilacs in the spring. At the hardware store, everyone knew you by name and where you lived. Going back toward home, the owner of the apothecary was completely in charge. We addressed him as Mr. All Our Drugs. When the babies came, he provided everything we needed into the wee hours of the night. Within a small, few-blocks-wide area, there was most anything one and one's family would want. The biggest treat, and one we partook in most every day, was meeting for lunch at Schrafft's, where we ate innumerable egg salad sandwiches. Then I would buy a yummy cheese bread to take home. I've never found one like it since. They weren't the most productive days, I must look back and say.

Before dinner parties, the local vendor I relied upon most was the florist. I always had an abundance of flowers all over the house. But for parties, the florist and I would hold summits.

I used one florist in particular, Flowers by Court, who knew me very well. I would spend the day there collaborating on extraordinary arrangements. Together, the florist and I devised terrines of riotous tulips in the dead of winter or filled an empty white birdcage in my dining room with lily of the valley as delicate as lace. We worked very hard at creating a unique tableau for each holiday, each dinner party. I didn't use vases or containers from the shop. Instead, I brought something out from my large collection of china and tableware as inspiration. If I purchased a new tablecloth embroidered with blue-and-white flowers, out came my blue-and-white china and perhaps blue hydrangeas and white lilies for my opulent glass epergne.

It was wearing. In my day, all my married friends, me included, tried to outdo one another. It became very competitive, but in all honesty I always won. Hosting was bred into me by my mother. I loved her dinner parties. She had marvelous taste, and I tried to emulate her in every way, even if I didn't want to think that was what I was doing. Unconsciously, that's most likely why I painted my dining room in Wedgwood blue, hung chinoiserie drapes of blue birds and branches on a white background, and filled the hutch with blue-and-white ceramics. My mother adored blue and white.

Unlike my mother, I am an introvert—really, the lady behind the door. This, too, stoked my sense of achievement in setting a beautiful table where, all without speaking, one can express artistry and welcome guests. During my younger life, I so often fantasized about overseeing the kitchen, fixing the table, seeing to it that everything was perfect, and then walking out and shutting the door. I absolutely wanted to labor over the preparations for a luxurious evening but would have much preferred to leave before it began. Instead, I had to swallow my fears along with the soup and entertain our guests while my husband, Sonny, the ha-ha guy, drank.

Although the drinking caused so many fights in my marriage, and I no longer drink, I still love the bar we built in the apartment. It really is a very unsophisticated bar, built into a closet nook in the den when we moved in. I might add that some of the bottles, both opened and sealed, remain even today! Vintage booze. All the crystal cut-glass decanters are lined up, and the silver ice bucket holds a pair of tongs, although it hasn't been filled with ice for quite some time. The shelves above hold glasses of all shapes. I like that some don't match. There's something uncontemporary about it. Out of these collections from years ago, my favorites are my grandmother's Delft coasters and a silver decanter in the shape of an old whiskey bottle.

This is all from my old life. Sonny is gone and so are all the friends we used to have over, but the crystal finger bowls in which people really dipped their fingers and the silver ashtrays that went on each table remain. Today's world has changed so much from my days as a wife. You don't need any of the above for takeout.

I should take a page from my mother, who minimized before she died. Sonny and I moved my mother from the brownstone she loved into an apartment around the block in a new high-rise facing Lake Michigan—and she hated, *hated* it. She said it was too small and that she had never lived in a one-bedroom apartment. Though it was charming, and blue and white—done with Bruce Gregga's wonderful taste—she never really loved it there. When anyone walked in and invariably exclaimed how wonderful the view was, Mother always said, "I don't like looking out of windows." And she didn't. The refrigerator contained a five-pound can of coffee, champagne, Sara Lee coffee cake, maybe a jar of caviar, and peanut butter. Nothing to make or put together a meal. She sold all the stuff from the old house. By then her beloved bookstore took up most of her time, so she didn't really care about the domestic side of life anymore.

Living in a large apartment alone, surrounded by a lifetime of things with memories attached, I have gone the other route. I never changed my environment. Everything in the apartment remains the same as it was when we were a family.

There is one big exception—my clothing closets. A small college in Chicago that has archives of vintage clothing and came highly recommended by a friend chose to take a whole group from my wardrobe. I gathered together twenty or more dresses, hats, some lingerie, gloves, and packed them off for college! I'm so pleased they went to my hometown. Some of the pieces even had Chicago labels. Whatever comes of them, at least they went home.

I know I should be getting rid of so much more, otherwise I won't be around to see where all my things end up. I wish others would come and denude me of some, for it is such an effort to do it myself—and a very emotional one. There are several reasons for this, including the fact that I don't like disruption.

It doesn't occur to me to disrupt my possessions. I have liked orderliness all my life. Years ago, I wouldn't go to bed if an ashtray was still full. Now I can't if a glass is unwashed. No. I need everything in its place. When a guest leaves my apartment, I instantly puff up the cushions squashed by their presence. There is one notable exception to my tidying-up obsession. Each time I open the doors to a cabinet filled with old photographs, writing, and memorabilia, I quickly close it. Something very deep in my being keeps me out of the cabinet that houses a great deal of my past.

There is a way to make de-acquisitioning less chore and more celebration. In the last few years, I have been carefully going through my large collection of china and silver—and for a Christmas holiday, birthday, or any occasion when the spirit moves me (or more likely, thought strikes me), take a piece down from its shelf, polish it, wrap it, and give it to a special friend.

These are items in prime shape and in no way ready to be thrown away. But the question is: Is the person going to feel the way about what they receive that I feel about what I am giving? Because these things are very precious to me, or I wouldn't be hoarding them. I don't keep junk. But you can't control what other people feel or think, nor would I want to if I could. It makes *me* feel good to give them a treasure from my life.

I try to give things away every holiday. I even count Valentine's Day. (But *not* Halloween, which I have loathed since I was a little girl.) Special occasions give me an impetus to go into the drawers, find something for a person who will understand it, and package it up. I recently collected a huge bag of pins I bought at an antique fair a hundred years ago to give as a birthday present to my dear friend Edward Bess. Chock full of stuff that we used to consider junk but is not saleable, the bag must weigh at least five pounds! What were they doing in my drawer other than looking at me? Now Edward can collect or resell them. At least they'll go on into the world.

You need not wait for New Year's or St. Patrick's Day to make someone feel special. As you're cleaning a drawer or the closet, if you happen upon a piece of jewelry or clothing that you haven't worn in an age, and it makes you think of a friend or colleague, give it to them. It doesn't have to be anything costly. If you hand a friend a beautifully wrapped package on an ordinary day, they will have more time and energy to appreciate it than if it were a holiday. Maybe they'll really like it; maybe they won't. Either way, it will be from you, and that is meaningful.

Even better, one should have a party: spread everything out, fill a room, invite those you love and would like to come to take and enjoy! That is truly a dream.

*I like to rearrange — I do not like to get rid of!!*

NO ONE HAS SEEN IT ALL

# There's No Greater Luxury Than Linens

I OPENED A CHEST OF DRAWERS AND IT HAPPENED TO BE full of linens—acres of them! Beautifully wrapped in tissue, tablecloths yards long, napkins to match, doily sets, linens so ornately handprinted or embroidered they could be wall hangings, you name it—a past unfolding in front of me.

Linens were a favorite pastime of my mother, who ordered items for me whenever she ordered them for herself, which was quite a lot. From monogrammed handkerchiefs to place mats with lacework, Mother was truly obsessed. Consequently, I have drawers bursting at the seams with a range of table linens from mini to so immense there isn't an ironing board large enough to accommodate them.

It's not often anymore that you see linen tablecloths, napkins, and place mats, all beautifully pressed and coordinated with the china. I can think of one exception to the naked table that is today's fare: a longtime friend who invites me to her home a block away on Park Avenue for the Thanksgiving holiday every year. A hostess in the old mold, she sets the table for the large gathering with exquisite crisp linens. When the feast is finished, however, she sends everything out to be cleaned and folded. That's a great extravagance. I always had everything done at home, but that time is long gone. There is no greater luxury than linens—and no greater upkeep.

There's nothing more beautiful to me than a basket full of clean linens all pressed and starched. Other than for the very large table linens that went off to the very expensive hand laundry, we had a lovely woman, Isabelle, who washed and starched all the clothes, napkins, and tablecloths. She laundered and pressed my husband's shirts piled high from a week's worth of wear. Isabelle even starched my daughter's dresses and returned them pristine to Kathy's own small hangers.

I wonder if people appreciate the maintenance that goes into using real cloth when most choose paper or nothing at all. But that's not why you put care and time into lining up the scalloped edges of a cotton napkin with a plate. You do it for self-appreciation. There's a reward in elevating the experience by creating something out of the ordinary.

Then I remember: tomorrow is laundry day. It is truly a marvel how many towels one person can use!

# How to Iron a Napkin

IT'S NOT EASY AND SOMETIMES I GET ANGRY. WHEN I STILL drank, I would usually have a drink and put the radio on after bringing out the ironing board. Now I have to settle for the radio alone. I dampen the napkin with my hands and roll it, so it gets sopped. I like everything crisp, so I add spray starch although it isn't nearly as good as the old-fashioned starch that you used to boil. I've been known to put napkins in the freezer after wetting them, which replaces the starch. I use a steam iron. (I really need a new one.) After ironing, I fold the napkin. I don't press the folded napkin with the iron as some do because I like the napkin to stay light. The napkins I used in my old life I keep with my other linens for table settings. In the kitchen, I have a drawer with "everyday" napkins and place mats that I use for just me. They are washed and pressed to sit snugly on a tray. I never want to give up living like a person.

# Air Between the Hangers

YOU DON'T WEAR THE CLOTHES IN YOUR CLOSET UNLESS they're out and facing you. They practically need to speak to you. If not, they simply sit in the back, mixed up and mixed out of your everyday go-to garments.

If I had to name one of the greatest luxuries I possess, it wouldn't be my designer purses in rare skins or drawers full of filigreed silver flatware. It would be my empty closet. Yes, you did not misread. I have something very few people (and possibly no New Yorker) can claim—so much closet space that one sits completely empty. My apartment has an unusual number of walk-in closets: at least six, not counting the laundry room. Like so many other elements of my life, my closet space is a relic of the past. Apartments are simply not made this way anymore. You're lucky if you get one large closet that must be multipurpose for multipeople. Whole industries of storage contraptions have sprung up to remedy the problem.

I do believe most persons like to hear about my closet therapy! They for one cannot believe how many closets I inhabit. At one time we were a family—husband, two children, and household help inhabiting the rooms and filling the closets. That is long gone, and I have since spread out, which is a bad thing to do because we all tend to accumulate too much. I did empty my fur closet (I wouldn't even be able to stand up under the weight of the coats I used to own). It has become a set piece, a walk-in closet that holds only three fur-lined winter coats. Imagine! I have found something to occupy the shelves above: a collection of baskets that I cannot part with. It occurred to me that at Christmas I might fill them and give them to those who might appreciate and not throw away! In my everyday coat closet in the hallway, orderly and mundane, I always keep extra coat hangers for guests, who are few and far between of late.

On to the clothing closets. In one, dresses are hung on a high rod in the back, while a low rod in front houses jackets. Years ago, when we moved into the apartment, we built shoe doors, second interior doors on the closets that hold my shoes in neat rows from the top of the door to bottom. One holds evening shoes from another era. At this point, they are entirely decorative. The shoe doors work like a dream because there are no shoes on the floor. I should put that in the past tense. My sneaker collection, which has grown as has everyone's, is on the floor. But I stand them upright against the wall of the closet so they do not take as much room as they would if you placed them flat.

In another closet, my pants are on one side of the rod, and on the other are shirts and more shirts. On each side are shelves with storage boxes holding T-shirts and light sweaters for under jackets. Cardigan sweaters are separated mostly by color and occasion: those for the office, leisure, country, weekend wear. I like and demand order, and this helps me grab, dress, and run, which is what I do most workdays. Getting dressed can be a big bore day to day if you have to think too much about it.

In the same shirt closet, the two shelves above house handbags, all standing side by side in two neat rows (larger satchels on top, dressier ones on the second shelf). Again, easy to grab and run. Honestly, though, I don't change my handbag often. I'm "married" to a very light and washable canvas bag with a zipper. It is like my good luck charm.

My clothes are grouped by season: spring–summer and fall–winter. When one season is in operation, the other is snugly housed in a large, long closet I had built for just that and nothing else. Inside, a long shelf where I now keep some luggage used to hold hatboxes—clear ones so you could choose the desired hat without having to go through them all.

The changeover from one season to another is taxing but rewarding. Years ago, when I was more mobile, I tried on everything that came out of hibernation, giving away what looked dated or no longer fit. There were always many piles, but all orderly. Organizing one's wardrobe this way does take many hours and tremendous lifting power. It involves a great deal of pulling and rehanging, putting together pants, shirts, dresses, and skirts so they hang in kind. But when I change my closets over with the season, it's as if I'm seeing many of my clothes for the first time. Even the decades-old can appear new and unworn.

As I've oft repeated, busywork wards off the fear of loneliness. And closets offer multitudes in the way of busywork, no matter the time of the year. A favorite pastime of mine is redoing or sorting out. It's kind of how I run my business—tidy! Distracting from a dark mood is not the only reason, however. Every so often, I rearrange my pieces to change what is in front of me for quick organized dressing.

Many of us tend to wear the same thing day in and day out. As a society, we've become lackadaisical when it comes to dressing. We don't get very innovative unless maybe we're compelled by a special event, like a wedding or, more likely in my case, a funeral. In general, though, it's become far too easy to throw on one of the few outfits you've decided are *comfortable*. Think of digging into your closet as a treasure hunt. The reward can be great. For example, after unearthing an ancient double-faced brown jacket with a purple self-faced lining, I was stopped by many in the store with a "how beautiful."

One thing I can assure you of is that you will never get off the path of least resistance if you can't locate any other route. I make sure everything can be eyed, even my pantyhose—housed in the dresser containing lingerie, T-shirts, and socks. I roll my stockings up into doughnut configurations so they can be plucked from the drawer as easily as, well, a doughnut. I might mention that each drawer holds a quilted fabric drawer liner that the clothes rest upon. Nightgowns I don't wear anymore (but can't let go of) are tied neatly with grosgrain ribbon. My wedding nightgown with its chiffon straps peeks out from under the bow. I own so many scarves, as scarves always fit, no matter how the body changes. They are folded in half, facing you as you open the drawer, so that you can lift one out without disturbing all the others.

I also keep my extensive jewelry collection in a dresser drawer. What lies in it? A very fun, eclectic mix from a lifetime of looking. I have silver pieces of all varieties on a wire necklace, which is exceptional. The assortment goes back to my Chicago days, and that alone tells the story. Piles of Bakelite bracelets are threaded on the cardboard cores that once held paper towels. There is a profusion of pins: silver, gold, costume, anything one could imagine. At one time I collected wooden pins, mostly of animals and fish. I use these quirky pieces more than my precious jewelry. Known for my lapel pins, I usually go to the above drawer, pull out some plastic, wood, or even tin pin and wear it on my jacket or sweater.

It's a throwback to my mother, who always had on some sort of pin or necklace. No rings, however. Well, that's not entirely correct. My father purchased from a friend a sapphire cabochon ring, which she wore every day. I treasure and am ever so careful with the ring, as it was once "stolen." Many anguishing months after its disappearance, I found it back in its original resting place. I never learned where it had traveled, but all I cared about was its return. The ring was my mother's most favorite possession, as it is mine.

I was able to tell my mother's ring was missing only because I maintain the inventory in my closets and drawers. The days of overbuying and stashing away are over. We all have more than we need. Nothing should hide on a hanger in the back of the closet year after year. The passing of many seasons will not make you like a dress or jacket any better.

Be selective in your own closet. Use what you own. If you don't—give it away, get rid of it! Spare space is so fulfilling. It makes it so much easier to use what you have. No longer bogged down by the dross, dressing can become a light and inventive affair. My advice to all: if you see air between the hangers, you're in good shape.

# Host Dinner at Home, Even If You Don't Cook

I DON'T LIKE TAKEOUT. EXPENSIVE AND ARRIVING TO ONE'S door tepid, it is truly my pet peeve. Even opening the containers puts a damper on my appetite. To me, a fried egg and toast would suit my taste buds better than any delivery, no matter how gourmet the restaurant.

However, as with my nonuse of the cell phone, I recognize that I am severely outnumbered in this area. I may be the only person on earth who feels this way, as I have never met another. While I have always questioned the lack of cooking at home these days, I still encourage people to eat in their lovely, well-furnished homes they have put so much care and cost into.

Enjoy your very own surroundings. It is cozier and nicer to be with others in a home setting. Even if one doesn't like to cook—*gasp*—order in. Eat at your own table with your own dishes and maybe a candle or two. Romantic and warm, it's a fine way to be with family and friends.

# ON LIVING

# If I Worried About How I Was Going to Do Things, I Would Never Do Anything

I DO MOST EVERYTHING UNDER PRESSURE. THERE IS ALWAYS something standing in the way of perfection. That once hindered me from moving forward and achieving. Until, that is, I realized the entire world, without exception, is wrapped up in one package. No one is exempt. Everything comes and goes at a steady pace, so you must move forward to the next or be left behind. That is pressure enough.

# Find Strength, Even Under a Rock

I AM A DISCIPLINED SLEEPER. *ROLL OVER AND KEEP YOUR eyes closed!* is usually my motto. Not last night, though. All things crept into my brain, like my marriage. As much as I pushed the image away, Sonny appeared and reappeared. He wasn't the only one. Others I have known over the years crept in, all deceased, all the same type—in a word, unattainable. Not one could have been ready or able to have a simple, romantic, successful relationship.

Choosing that type has always been one of my weaknesses; consequently, nothing changed in the romantic part of my life, ever. I take full responsibility One side of me was drawn to difficult relationships, a turmoil that the night was full of.

Maybe it wasn't all my fault, in the sense that I came from a family with a long history of division. I lived through my mother and father's divorce. (Harry Stoll, the man I called Daddy and the love of my mother's life, was not my biological father.) Although I was only three years old at the time of their divorce, I have felt it all these many years. Divorce was such a terrible word when I was growing up, and yet it described my entire family. I was deeply embarrassed to acknowledge that my maternal grandparents and granduncle were also divorced.

Sadly, there are so many holes in the stories behind all this heartache. I'm not privy to what happened between the couples or how the individuals made sense of it afterward. Instead, I caught snatches of conversations, such as about my grandmother departing on her own journeys, once with a doctor, I remember. Or my grandfather remarrying—to his secretary, no less. I will never know the truth behind this sad mystery that has lived within me all my life. Why the secrecy? By constitution I am not a secretive person. It often makes me calmer to get the truth out.

From my family experience, I came to believe that many of us are ready to settle—by that I mean to continue with the mistakes we choose and make. As I grow older, however, I see that the young are different, courageous, more independent than my generation. Although I am long out of the game, I applaud them from the sidelines.

One can't blame others for unhappiness or discontent. Some people suffer through bad marriages, filled with anger, discontent, affairs, alcohol, and many other different ways out. Isn't it better to avoid the above and try to start a new life? It is not written in stone that you must suffer. Be brave. Move forward. Find strength, even under a rock.

*Our feelings are with us like our EYES – and LIMBS. They come Back in MANY guises Even as we grow older!!*

ON LIVING

# I Put Down the Drink

COMING OUT OF WORLD WAR II, EVERYONE WAS LOOKING for some kind of joyride. We all drank; at least that's how I remember it when I was a young woman. Sure, there were the goody-goodies, who didn't touch alcohol. But they were few and far between in the company Sonny and I kept. Our group went out nearly every weekend and many a weeknight, not to mention all the dinner parties at home where there was no shortage of cocktails. It was part of the fabric of society back then.

I used to drink to ease the anxiety. I have always lived with fear. It is my right hand, and I am left-handed. I was an excellent vodka drinker. In the old days at the store, we kept a bottle in the office that we occasionally pulled out at the end of an especially long day, often with the costume designers we worked hard with to find wardrobes for movies and television. If not, there was plenty of vodka at home, where I could pour a drink before the coat even came off. I never liked "to vodka" before 5:00 p.m. It was too easy to slip into the bottle during a long day at home.

Although fear has never left me, I quit drinking when I was ninety-three. I was frightened for my brain and its proper functioning. Alcohol-induced dementia is real. It was a question of me giving it up or it giving *me* up. I put the vodka down and said, "No more."

Once the idea occurs to me that it is time to give something up and I decide to move ahead with it, I don't give it a second thought. I quit smoking the same way. After I was diagnosed with breast cancer in the early 1990s, I swore off the cigarettes I had been smoking since I was thirteen. I did it of my own volition, not because anyone told me to. Perhaps it was also some sort of peace offering to a higher power if he let me survive the cancer. Anyway, I never missed it—or the vodka. I am lucky that way.

It is luck and certainly not courage, because the latter quality is in short supply in my being. Now, instead of vodka, I like to drink nonalcoholic beer when I get home. While out for dinner or in social situations, I have noticed that people tend to push alcohol on me when I attempt at politely passing. "Have a little drink!" they insist, drawing way more attention to the moment than it deserves. Why they can't leave it be is beyond me. I don't think anyone would badger me to eat a tuna sandwich or drink a soda if I didn't feel like it. I am not offended; I chalk it up to the busywork people make to divert themselves from their own problems. But I don't indulge them either. Instead, I throw out a one-liner that scares them to death.

"Go ahead. Looks like you need it more than me," I answer, and they disappear quickly.

Drinking is fun for some, medicine for others, poison for yet another group. Don't let ye olde peer pressure change the habits that are best for you. Your beverage shouldn't be the center of another's evening.

# My Favorite Publication

PEOPLE WOULD BE SURPRISED TO FIND OUT THAT MY favorite magazine isn't *Vogue* or *Town & Country*. I don't look at those magazines; I live that. Nope! It's actually the catalog from the Vermont Country Store. I like things that have to do with the home, and this business that's been family owned since 1946 is very homey. Even when I was a single workingwoman, I never gave up the thought of being a homemaker of sorts. Their mail-order service has everything from kitchen wax to leather book weights to Dresdner Stollen (the fruit bread with rum-soaked sultanas and candied lemon and orange peels comes in a beautiful tin and makes for a wonderful gift for the out-of-towners on your Christmas list). The clothes portion doesn't interest me, although some of the nightgowns and flannels are worth flipping the page. Simply put: the Vermont Country Store is not pretentious, and in my life I've found "not pretentious" to be two of the most pleasing words in my vocabulary.

# In My Next Life I Hope to Be a Farmer

THE FIRST THING PEOPLE NOTICE WHEN THEY COME INTO my office is my window facing the park, and the second is the plants that thrive happily on the sill. My showy orchid collection has oft been cited in profile pieces written about me over the years. It started with one orchid plant and then another and on and on. Although often in bloom, they require little care. I have always thought their good health is because they like the company in the office.

The orchids have many friends. Over the years, I have grown all sorts of flora—violets, mint, any old plant someone could no longer or never was able to care for. Call me the matron of an orphanage, as I really do consider them my children.

I am the third generation of women who favored flowers and plants over people. My grandmother was mad for violets, keeping her violet plants on the window ledge and smothering herself in violet perfume. My mother always had something—perhaps a gardenia or any other seasonal flowering pot—blooming in the window of her bookstore. Every spring, she put planters in the front with petunias (white only) and geraniums that bloomed until fall. It was definitely her garden.

The odd thing is, despite my deep and abiding love of plants, I have never had my own garden. In all the houses Sonny and I rented while we were married, there was never a place to plant a proper garden. Summers spent on Long Island when the children were small were occupied looking at the ocean with beach club friends. Oh, we were very social in those days. Cabana "pals" would haul out the booze at five, and we would watch the sunset as the beach emptied of people. We dressed up on Saturday nights for outdoor buffet dinners and dancing at a local country club. I rather liked it, even though I was going through husband trouble. In those silly days there was always someone's husband who would take a fancy to me and ask to "trip the light fantastic." Nothing ever happened after the music stopped, but the flirtation made me feel pretty, young, and desirable.

I suppose it's no wonder I never tended to vegetation at the shore. Even if we had rented a home with a garden, between sunset cocktails and swing dancing, there was hardly time to coax anything from the earth. Later we purchased a lake house in the Berkshires, and although the terrain was very different, our routine was quite similar. In the summer, we left New York every Thursday with the dog on my lap panting to go and our cook, Frieda, in the back seat. Sonny was always ready, sitting behind the wheel, anxious to be off. I on the other hand was not. To me it meant company, many meals, shopping, preparing. Strange, isn't it, that I didn't take refuge in a vegetable or flower garden? Not really. The house my husband insisted we buy was on a hill with a walkway spiraling down to the lake—rocky and difficult to plant anything unless you were an acrobat.

I fantasize about plants and flowers, but most of all my true love is the vegetable stands. My daughter feels the same and partakes in a big way. Now that I no longer travel like I used to, jealous am I. I yearn to see the vegetable stands in the Hamptons, where the fertile loam soil warmed by the surrounded seawater brings forth corn sweet to bursting, starchy clean potatoes, lettuces so beautiful you could use them instead of flowers in an arrangement, cheerful sunflowers, and so much more. The bounty is enough to fill its own book.

I once loved to stop along the highway, to buy but also to take in all the growing things visually. It's a treat for me like no other. For those who take them for granted—I wish them to partake. I would take a June strawberry fresh from the field over a fancy-dress cocktail party at a beachfront abode any day of the week.

Of those I see packing up their cars with the aid of the doormen for weekends in the country (leaving my apartment building quite empty, I must add), the clients in need of summer-weight sweaters for a last-minute trip to the Cape, or the friends rushing off to their second homes, I often wonder, *Do any of them ever lie on a lounge and just look up, inhale the fresh air, hear the nature noises all around?*

I am a cloud watcher from childhood. I can remember lying on the grass in a Chicago park looking up, conjuring all sorts of guesses as to what forms the clouds mimicked. As a young person I knew and learned in elementary school every cloud name. It is still a pastime I often indulge in from my wonderful window in my office. I am mesmerized by their size and many formations—sometimes faces, animals, buildings, and numerous everyday things. They are my fantasy and take me slightly out of the real world.

My window also blesses me with a front-row seat for each season, from spring's earliest buds to my favorite, fall, when nature puts on a real show. I love the greening of every leaf and bursting of each bulb. Upon my arrival early morning after a snowfall, the world is wrapped in snow. The entire park is a complete white fairyland, with every tree coated in snow as if someone had painted each branch. The vast ever-changing scene from my window saves me from so much inner thought.

It has always amazed me that people believe Park Avenue is so glorious. From my apartment, I face another building with mostly drawn shades. In a word: gloomy. During the pandemic, I often thought of taking a chair out to the avenue's central mall to sit under one of its cherry trees and admire the tulips or begonias. In my next life I hope to be a farmer. Until then, I have to content myself with being friends with one.

Duanne, a farmer in the prairies of western Canada, started writing to me, and we've been pen pals ever since. He gives me news about the harvest: "We have been going like fiends to get the crop in and are down to our last two hours. Not only did we run out of room, but rain has added to the delay." Or his pet fox, Jules: "I have to stop feeding him dog food though. Getting looks from the boys." Or his couture business (oh, yes, this farmer moonlights as a dressmaker, or perhaps it's the other way around): "I had to keep the shop open longer than I had planned. But as of last week, the last gown I made went out, and the door will be shut for a while or at least until the proverbial dust settles from harvest. (This is causing me to wonder about something. Do you think Ralph Lauren is as hands-on on his farm? I'm leaning toward no.)" How I relish his news about the health of the cattle or photos taken with his phone from the tractor of the fields at daybreak.

I have very little patience, but one thing I use and hold on to for sanity and peace is my love and appreciation for all things green. Those of you who are still of the able-bodied persuasion, take time to find that green grass and that tree to sit under and reflect. It does wonders for the mood.

*Persons have short memories. In my ninty-six years of living I've often had to remind them we did this – we lived that – and we thought this and that! We've been through that already!*

# All Virtues Have a Limit

AT THIS POINT IN MY LIFE, I AM PERHAPS MOST LAUDED FOR coming to work every day. I understand a ninety-six-year-old who continues to clock into the office is a marvel, not unlike a circus act. However, my feat of wonder is not thanks to any special talent; rather, it is just force of discipline. Getting up early and going to the office is my saving grace; the many phone calls don't get me out of the apartment. The minute I put the key in my office door, I am distracted from inner feelings I don't care to engage.

That much-lauded trait, discipline, can have its ugly side, as all things do. As much as I try to restrain myself, I am a perfectionist. The impulse rises with me early in the morning. In the way some pray to the Lord or meditate, I go about my daily chores, starting with my bed. I cannot, never have, will never leave my bed unmade (without a crease). Then I tidy up so when I come home after work everything is just as I am used to. When I close my front door, ride the elevator, and step out onto the avenue to head to work, my obsession accompanies me. I am calmed by an orderly office: everything by appointment, all calls answered by end of day, coffee table books by friends and chairs lined up.

I recognize this is probably a mental illness. A horrible trait, the need for order at all costs and at all times causes so much unrest and dissatisfaction. I become unnecessarily bothered by and immersed in things, no matter how big or small. A perfect example: the reading lamp next to my bed fell off the wall during a Fourth of July weekend, creating mayhem. A broken lamp on the wall next to my bed needs repair, and I want it done and finished immediately! Never mind that the building's super does not work on weekends, let alone holidays. But that is how everything is for me: what appears to be a lack of patience is fear settling in and making the situation harder to deal with. I fretted all weekend until the task was accomplished on Monday.

There is a limit to the power of all virtues, and when they exceed that threshold, they enter the territory of vice. While I have not had much success, stay on the right side of the boundary line.

# The Silver Lining in Not Finding the Silver Lining

IF SOME OF WHAT I'VE SHARED WITH YOU SOUNDS VERY pessimistic, that is because I am a pessimist by nature and my fear is of what is to come. I guess I don't want to be disappointed. Nonetheless, it often doesn't sit well with people I know. I have always been jealous of those who can find a silver lining. My background also didn't furnish one. It was all on the doubtful side of the equation. However, in my aged life it has helped me, and made me more aware and cautious.

Is there any way to prepare for the unknown? Regardless of our circumstances, we never know what to expect. I have lived through a lot of history and can say with authority that today we are living through a dizzying period in which no one knows what is going to happen day to day. I can also say, despite all my worrying, we are never, ever prepared for tomorrow. I don't care how intelligent or prepared you are. No exceptions.

In other words, whatever happens—so be it. Join in and enjoy the time. Take it from a pessimist.

# Honesty Gets Me Through a Great Deal

IT HAD BEEN SUCH A LONG TIME BETWEEN HAIRCUTS THAT I took scissors to my locks and got caught by the man who has cut my hair for years. "Did you do a number on this side of your hair, Betty?" I didn't need to say a word; my expression—and yes, my coif—said everything. I could never have been a robber, grifter, or in any profession that requires disguise and duplicity. I would always be caught. Although it embarrasses me to no end to call a host with regrets, I will never, ever make up a story or tell a lie. This is something I will not do under any circumstances.

In reflection, my honesty has gotten me through a great deal. I look people right in the eye and tell them how it is. For sure, sometimes it doesn't work. But then you can't have everything go your way 100 percent of the time. When it comes to selling clothes, my honesty is famous, or infamous. I am known to utter "take it off" often before a client has both arms in the sleeves if the garment doesn't fit, the color is off, or the person doesn't need it. I do it with complete honesty, as if I were the client. I remember when I was in my other life and a salesperson would start to press me. I lost interest completely. My candor has been successful and brought me many cheers of recognition.

ON LIVING

Truthfulness can be uncomfortable or anxiety making in the moment. You may even face anger. In the long run, however, you will receive more respect than ire. And, best of all, you'll sleep soundly.

*I have NEVER wanted to Be anything more than what I am.*

# ON SOLITUDE

# A Strange Animal

I WILL OPEN UP A CHAPTER THAT HAS BEEN CLOSED FOR A long while—depression. Today it has left me, but oh, those years I wore it like a scarf.

Connected to loneliness, depression plagued me as a child raised in a small, not-too-close family in which two of its three main members—Mother and Father—were often "on the go." I grew up through *the* Depression, a world war, divorce, death. I imagine it must have been a great deal to endure and, most of all, understand. In those days when "children were seen and not heard," we small people had a double way of existing. I don't recall any conversations or heart-to-hearts with my parents, but I do remember the heartaches, fears (many), and feelings of insecurity about my intelligence, looks, and social scene. Alone in my room, I did my best to cope but didn't always succeed.

Depression is a strange animal that stalked me into young adulthood and marriage. In creeped a rather low and lazy mood—almost to the point of being sleepy. When this happened, the desolation would build up until I entered a faraway state where I listened to others with only half an ear. With little interest in what they were saying, I answered in a derogatory way. Not very nice. Sometimes I became angry. Even less nice. I was often disapproving. If they said yay, I said nay. The truth was I was defeated before I had even tried.

Without a doubt, my greatest therapy was entering the job world. As frightened as I was of the new learning experience in my forties, I trudged on and allowed those I trusted to help me find the real person within. They saw something I did not see or never bothered to dig for. Somehow, I made it to ninety-six and am still here on the broom!

If you are low to the point of hopeless, let stronger folk pull you out. Even if you can't or won't believe that things will get better, that you have something inside worth tugging on, let yourself be fooled until it comes true.

*When you are an only child, to whom do you talk but yourself??*

# Life Has Many Chapters

THERE WAS A TIME WHEN EVERY DAY WAS SOAP OPERA DAY at the store. The costumers for the programs, like *One Life to Live*, *All My Children*, *General Hospital*, and on and on: they couldn't get enough clothes. The shows were daily and full of scenarios from parties to deathbed scenes. Although not too intellectual, daytime television was brilliant in the way it appealed to all ages, from college kids to their grandmothers. It also used clothes like we eat three meals a day. Price was no object. In other words, it was glorious fun. The various costume designers and I became good friends. Many an evening did we hoist a few and laugh about what we did in the day. Sadly, so many of them are gone now—not just from the business but from this Earth! It was a wonderful, creative period in my life. They were true creators, artistic and *intellectual*. I truly miss their friendships, but that is another chapter. As I keep writing, I am beginning to realize how many chapters in my life were learning ones. Consider the chapter you are in and what you can read from it, whether that's meeting new types of people, gaining skills, or overcoming fears. And know that, sooner or later, you'll turn the page.

ON SOLITUDE

# A Lifeline to the World

I AM BLESSED. MY PHONE RINGS FROM MORNING TO EVENING. In the store and at home. Clients from the present. People from the past—and my how long my past is! Now I receive calls from the children of my oldest long-gone friends, now grandparents themselves.

In my apartment, I use an old Princess phone. I have two of the little white phones, one in the den that I use all the time and another in my bedroom right next to the bed. No call waiting, no voicemail function, they are positively archaic. I'm okay with that because I don't like anything I have to learn how to use. It is a phenomenon that I don't use a cell phone. Consequently, I don't spend my days flipping through photos, looking through the contraption at some distortion of reality. Everyone urges me to update myself. I don't have Netflix either. Long ago, a friend brought me a cordless phone that sits in my kids' room. I've never used it. Not once. I'm not interested. My mind says to me, "You've gotten along without for all these years; hold that close to your being."

I do talk on the phone, however. My phonebook of forty-plus years is evidence. A jumble of information, it contains my old and new life. A friend suggested that the secret to my success is simply that I "pick up the phone." I don't have a great feeling for the notion that I am any kind of success. I bristle against the word *legendary*. I'm not in awe of my own publicity and do not confuse it with companionship. But as to my friend's suggestion, yes, I am always available. You can engage me on anything.

Although I never disconnected from it, the pandemic helped many of us learn to reconnect on the phone. One devoted friend called to recount how a bird had gotten into her home. She and her husband broomed their way through a large house to free the poor thing. I believe the simple creature was carrying a message for a very disciplined wife and mother: ultimately, we can't control everything.

A dear, ever-so-smart woman who worked for me twenty-odd years ago, newly widowed, fled to her house in the country. She has taken to watching her three great sons chop down a favorite tree and turn it into a very large conference table.

Another friend calls each day to tell me in great depth what she is about to cook. Her desire is to whet the appetite of her family members, a diversion I would say. She delves into exotica, and I love every minute.

At home one evening I was brushing my favorite sweaters—Libertine—when the phone called me away, and by God it was Johnson Hartig—Libertine himself checking on me! The genius behind the eclectic fashion line is one of my favorite people in the world. We talked of his kitchen garden and the steps and fireplace he was tackling with a blue-and-white spongeware

ON SOLITUDE

process. (I love love china spongeware.) The delightful diversion took me away from sadder, lonelier thoughts.

An example: I was very attached to my therapist—Philip. We first met sixty-plus years ago, when I was desperate. I didn't eat or sleep. I didn't function in any way. Literally at my wits' end. A breakdown sent me to "the institution," in this case, Payne Whitney. Upon my release, the facility sent me to Philip. No excuses: his office was a block from the apartment. My first impression was: *He is not for me; I'll never be able to sit in a chair facing him.* I did not want to go on to another day, but he insisted on pulling me back into the real world.

To make a long story short, I stayed in therapy for many years. When I started working at Bergdorf Goodman, we saw each other less frequently. I kept returning to that chair, however. A bout of cancer, my husband's death, all the bad stuff sent me back to find strength. Philip was always welcoming. I felt he was very proud of me and my accomplishments.

When he moved to a nursing home, I struggled to find the courage to call him there.

My what you can do with a head trip. When I climb into bed, I think my ears are about to fall off. I count on my fingers how many persons have bothered to find my phone number and thank God for it.

Conversation can get repetitious, particularly at my age. I don't like when people nitpick, such as a dear friend who in today's calls complained at length that she couldn't find

Pellegrino or fresh berries in the market. Perhaps I'm sensitive being a member of the service industry myself.

In my other life I used to call in orders every day from the butcher, vegetable market, and grocery store. Wife and mother, I planned and fretted. Would the guests eat the roast if cooked rare? Would the children try the creamed spinach? The people who answered, Jack, Mike, Alonzo, were well-known to me and vice versa. They knew my voice upon picking up. It's only all these years later I recognize that at the store where I work, I'm on the other end of the phone.

The phone is a connection, but then so are the mop and broom. I try to reckon with my anger and be more benevolent. Not give up kindness. My old friend Sylvia Weinstock called me sometime before her death at ninety-one. It had been awhile since we'd spoken. All was well: children, new apartment (she sold her town house). Her prescription to me: "Have a vodka, Betty."

"It's too early," I retorted.

"Nonsense," she said. "We'll talk soon."

Click.

Every day or so, I learn of someone who has passed away. At the very start of the pandemic, Saturday, April 4, was a so-sad day for me. My friend of more than fifty years, Victor Skrebneski, died. He discovered a camera as a seven-year-old boy playing in our native Chicago (Victor turned the lost item in to the park attendant, but was allowed to keep it when no owner

ON SOLITUDE

returned) and went on to become an internationally sought-after photographer. A person with taste par excellence, he could walk into a room, "eyeball it," and the chair would be in another place, the room entirely changed.

His photographs for clients such as our beloved Marshall Field's were new at the time in '50s fashion. Starting in the '60s, he became well-known for his striking ads for Estée Lauder, on occasion taking the photos right in his own house on Chicago's North Side. But I loved his portraits of people—Orson Welles, Audrey Hepburn, Bette Davis, and many less famous. I own a most treasured one of my husband and me, in which I'm wearing a Pucci dress, one of the few garments I wish I hadn't given away.

Perhaps I knew Victor best as my mother's travel companion. He and his partner at the time, Bruce Gregga, escorted Mother throughout the world. The three tripped off to Europe and Mexico and across the United States, having crazy fun—vodka and caviar times.

That day, Bruce called from Santa Barbara, and we talked at length about Victor. Honestly, it wasn't sad. We talked and walked through the fun, good days spent together, building, growing. I was married with college-aged children then. We were crazy, bouncing between Bruce and Victor's home in Chicago and mine in New York.

One Christmas in the same apartment I'm writing from now, we were preparing for our large, decadent Christmas Eve open house. Victor arrived from Chicago the day before the party with Mother. They stopped by for a drink before supper at Le Veau d'Or, a favorite bistro on East Sixtieth Street. I was fixing the dining room with Christmas cheer when Victor decided to stand on the dining room table, scissors in hand, and garland the chandelier with fresh pine boughs, lights, and berries. Very beautiful. Wouldn't you know it, he blew the light circuit. Heaven help us in finding an electrician on Christmas Eve eve! God was on my side: my dear alcoholic super managed to piece us together, and all of us drank many a toast to him later. I could write a small novel based on our antics during that opulent time. There were no cares when we congregated.

Dear, dapper, handsome, talented-in-so-many-ways Victor! I used to call every few weeks, and he would fill me in on his cleaning out of all the photos from his ninety years on this earth. We made an old connection, warped in time, new until the end.

Do not forget the original intention of the phones that are attached to the palm of everyone's hand these days. It is to use your voice and listen to others. Use this healing magic as often as you can.

*Everything good or Bad has an ending. And Then a new Beginning.*

ON SOLITUDE

# I Never Miss a Meal

IT IS A DREARY OCTOBER SUNDAY. THE WEATHER, SOMEwhere between cloudy and a light rain, is loathed by most, particularly on a weekend. I relish a good day to hunker down and straighten drawers and closets or cook warm, rich-smelling soup. Most of all, it is the kind of weather in which one doesn't feel guilty not going outside into the world.

I have a meat loaf I made in the oven. The recipe—which calls for a pound of "ground pig" as well as chicken livers, spinach, and allspice—was written down more than half a century ago in the three-ring binder where I keep recipes from countless meals. This particular recipe book was my invention. While my mother and grandmother rarely entered the kitchen, I have always loved that part of the house best. To this day, I find the kitchen, and all it offers, to be a welcome place.

I was brought up eating meals in the kitchen with the people I loved, Irish women my mother employed in my parents' home on the South Side of Chicago. I spent so much time with the "ladies of the kitchen," who cooked and baked to perfection. All through my childhood, I watched the pots boiling, and on occasion was allowed to lend a hand, or finger. A particular favorite was coconut cake with homemade marshmallow frosting and fresh grated coconut, perhaps because I was allowed to help hammer open the coconut, catch the milk, and then grate the meat on an old-fashioned grater. Sometimes a bit of blood escaped into the mixture.

Our pantry was as magical to me as my grandmother's closet, where I played dress-up. I loved pickle season, when a huge crock of small cucumbers sat by the pantry's window, which kept it cool for just the right fermenting. There were shelves with oilcloth on them where marmalade and jellies also fermented. It was spectacular, and as a little girl I would visit often, if only to poke my fingers in the dill pickle bin. Oh, and the best shelf, sweet pickle slices, called bread and butter pickles (no one knows why). Next to them would be corn relish, made when the corn was in ripe season. Another shelf held—my favorite to this day—Concord grape jelly. Next to it, my mother's favorite, tomato jam. Each season, something new was added. Summer was tomatoes. At Christmas, orange and sugar. Pickled peaches with cloves poked into them were served with yummy pot roast and potato pancakes in the fall! Although it was so very long ago, I remember each preserve like it was yesterday.

I continued my love affair with the kitchen early on in my marriage. Although I was never a baker, I adored making brisket, soups, and first courses. I decided to create a recipe book in a three-ringer binder. Matzo balls from the '40s; roast duck and sauerkraut from the '60s; my dear friend Susie's chicken, browned with white wine and cider vinegar; a simple mustard sauce that consists of nothing more than butter, flour, light cream, a little sugar, and Gulden's! Most are written in my trademark black marker pen on college-ruled paper now yellowed with time. Some, like Maine scallop salad, are clipped from the newspaper. Shirley Glaser—the wife of the famous graphic designer and *New York Magazine* founder Milton Glaser and an artist in her own right—kindly typed up her divine recipe for pappa al pomodoro. After marrying, the pair spent a few years living in Italy, where perhaps she picked up this recipe for the most marvelous use of stale bread.

My old recipe book goes untouched now. I don't cook as I used to—dinner parties for a dozen or more took a full week of preparation between our cook, my dear Frieda, and me. That isn't to say I don't cook. On the contrary: dinner is a full course meal; on weekends, real breakfasts with eggs. My meals today are simpler, but something is always available. Today, being late to the game, I made a quick tomato-bean soup with herbs. That will keep the week. I will sauté some thin pork chops with onion, breaded—enough for two meals. I also made a salad with herbs and olives. I keep lots of greens, arugula being a particular favorite. I also always have hard-boiled eggs on hand to use in a pinch. I found an apple going soft and baked it with raisins in the toaster oven—good with yogurt. There are pears for a salad tomorrow with feta cheese and lettuce. This will keep me going for the workweek.

When I make recipes of old—such as the meat loaf I labeled "Kathy's pâté" in humorous homage to my daughter's love for the dish—I do not need to consult my book. I have made these dishes so many times, my hands work without need of measuring cups or a brain.

I personally believe a kitchen can tell you more about a person than, say, the clothes closet, which only shows how someone looks. The kitchen speaks to more than how you eat, to how you live. My cabinets and drawers are full of kitchen gadgets, ricers, slicers, dicers, some maybe used once before the thrill wore off; many bowls, large, small, wooden, glass, and porcelain; steamers, roasting pans, sieves, and—would you believe?—a dear possession, a black cast-iron stew pot that belonged to my great-grandmother and was lugged all the way from Chicago in 1947. It was used, cleaned, and reused many times in my past life, when Frieda kept it full and bubbly.

For me, food has always been an uplifter. Even during the rationing of most food during World War II, we found clever ways to reinvent and circumvent. I spent most of my life loving the kitchen—my warm refuge, declaration of womanhood, store of gratification.

My wealthy neighbors, on the other hand, don't seem to know what to eat. I no longer smell the delicious aromas wafting from the kitchens of apartments where, I liked to imagine, cooks of all varieties consulted recipes, sampled while they stewed, and ladled out their final creations. The building appears to be devoid of home cooks. Outside, what I see is not to be believed. Although many of my building's inhabitants escape every weekend and holiday to second homes in the Hamptons, Connecticut, Palm Beach, and beyond, heaping mounds of takeout containers arrive from every restaurant on the Upper East Side on weekends. The plastic-bag mountain will reach to the sky and beyond. These deliveries are for people who, according to my observations, continue to order in most of their meals. Looking out the window some evenings, even in snowstorms, all I see are the poor delivery people racing through red lights to transport those meals.

I have never picked up the phone for takeout. I do not order in food. I do not care for the quality. I've spoiled me.

Being alone is something I am quite used to by now. I could write articles on the situation. The thing about living alone that I find one needs to be overly careful about is eating habits. So many persons my age neglect their three-meal-a-day routine. Either they are not hungry or they forget. I do not give in to any of the above. I do not miss a meal. True, there is more care given to some meals than others. But I always make up for it, and usually at dinner.

I am very disciplined about my eating habits (as I am about most areas of life). My youth and upbringing are the foundation, I am sure. Childhood is in much of our daily makeup. As a young girl, I was never allowed to miss a meal, regardless of the time of day, or what the meal consisted of. It is no wonder that I grew into a fussy and particular ninety-six-year-old who has developed a very strict routine.

I visit the grocery store once a week with a list. Sunday is usually my shopping day. I don't like to stop in the store on my way home from work. That mode of purchasing often leads to buying something I already have in the cupboard. While it can be put to use at another time, I do not like waste and detest throwing food away. Remember, I lived through the years of World War II, when meat, butter, sugar, and more were rationed.

My grocery shopping is pretty well planned week by week. Upon returning from the supermarket, I set to unpacking. My refrigerator is very orderly, like my life, or most certainly my closets. I am always straightening both. I guess you could call them overorganized. If I'm not mindful, organizing them can become a second job.

Sundays are the day I not only shop but also cook for the week. As I said, I no longer spend long hours in the kitchen like I used to. I do not have the patience. I always have high hopes when I start a kitchen project, but lately I become distracted. I suspect it is because when I begin to realize I'm doing all this work for only one person—me—I'm dissuaded from moving on with the cooking project. But I must say I do not give up. I am much too frugal for that.

In fact, it is very important to my mindset not to give up preparing food, to have something to look forward to when I come home from work. Yes, I find it harder and harder to know what to prepare. Boredom seems to be the main dish of the moment. But being disciplined, I know I must eat: meat, vegetables, potatoes. A complete meal. Trying to hold on to good habits is not always so easy. Each day as I prepare my dinner, I remind myself of that.

No matter the menu—a chop or brussels sprouts and chestnuts (one of my favorite recipes, no more than a buttered baking dish, a bit of water, and salt and pepper)—the minute I arrive home, I head straight for the kitchen. There I keep a tray always at the ready with a dinner-size plate, and the proper silverware. It always sends the word to me to prepare a proper meal.

I am so loaded with china, silver, and so much more from my past life—including linens, closets full! I have never, ever used paper napkins. No matter how attractive they are, initials or whatever, I abhor them. So, each evening the tray is adorned with a linen place mat and matching napkin. I also use a proper glass, and if I'm having a salad, a separate salad plate as well. Dinner this way makes me feel very comfortable.

I eat with a bit of the past, including a pretty garnish. Back in my entertaining days, I delighted in making garnishes for the trays of appetizers. I cut produce—such as turnips, beets, or lemons—into the shape of flowers. Radishes were the easiest. Cut them all over and thrust them into water, and they open up flower like! I still do it, even if only for my own enjoyment.

The element of cooking that sends me most quickly back in time is the aroma from my dinner preparations. It takes me back first to the smell of food cooking when I arrived home from school. That meant Mother, Father, and I would have dinner together and I wouldn't have to eat alone in the kitchen. The next place it takes me is the smell of Frieda's cooking when I would walk in the door of my own apartment in the early evening. The apartment, then a real home with a family, smelled lived in. The lights were all turned on, and the children had been bathed. They too smelled so good. Those smells still linger in my head. Both my daughter and my son, John, are good and innovative cooks—as are my grandchildren. Kathy uses cooking as a grand hobby, while John is different: no meat, only vegetables and baked goods. I am pleased I have left some mark in their lives.

As I remove the bubbling meat loaf from the oven, the rich, tangy smell permeates the apartment and makes me feel normal. It harkens back to when the same apartment was occupied by many, the kitchen busy, lights always up, and the delicious smells a constant. The memories are of not only food but family. I am not very nostalgic. I try to stay away from it. However, without me even suspecting, thoughts sneak in. I can handle that.

*Soft cheese for dessert satisfies the sweet tooth.*

# Why I Sleep in a Single Bed

I'VE OFTEN WATCHED FRIENDS WHO HAVE HAD AN INVITATION to visit my bedroom—to go through my drawers, examine my closets, borrow a piece of jewelry, whatever—as they make their way to my beds. Yes, beds—two single beds with quilted bedspreads, pillow shams, skirts, the whole nine yards of the 1950s.

My mother and father had single beds: my mother propped on many pillows, a swinging light overhead, drinking her coffee, the toast on the tray under a dome to keep it warm. She never finished one piece. Father, a large man who, being a workaholic, could snore on any chair or couch or standing up, filled his bed top to toe, side to side.

Fast-forward to my marriage in 1945. I was terrified of New York. Why not? Our first apartment on Sixth Avenue was like living in the bus lane! There was never a thought of anything but single beds. No one even broached the subject. Linens were ordered and monogrammed. The singles were pushed together, making them look like one. In those days I would crawl into my husband Sonny's bed, cling to him in my fear and loneliness, and then return to my own—my hand within reach of the telephone. I used that phone from bed many times, calling "home" for consolation.

NO ONE HAS SEEN IT ALL

Apartments were difficult for everyone in the 1940s. You had to know someone to procure this scarce commodity. My sister-in-law lived in the Park Avenue building I still live in sixty-seven years later. A record—they should waive my rent as a prize! When Sonny and I first moved in, we would come home after being out until God knew what hour and drive behind the milkman and his horse and buggy. I'm dating myself for sure.

Still attached to my Chicago roots, I had the family decorator help with the apartment, and of course that included the two singles that still exist in my bedroom. Don't worry, reader. The mattresses have been renewed over the years. Sonny's twin next to mine has been vacant for forty years or more. The monogram night spreads that lie over the blankets are a bit worn but useable. Two pillows with cases matched to the sheets are changed twice a week—washed *and* ironed. Very old hat, but oh so nice to climb into, particularly in this somewhat awful world.

The intimate aspect of single beds I am sure one must question. Sexually, how do two manage? Well, we did, and children were produced from its intimacy. However, after the lovemaking process, one's partner would depart to his own bed. That rather broke the spell, which was neither good nor bad. It just was.

A little distance can paradoxically create more closeness. The distance between Sonny's bed and mine could grow to a small gulf or shrink to nothing at all depending on how we were feeling. No matter how bitterly we had argued, there wasn't a night that went by when I didn't reach out from my bed to his in order to hold his hand and say "God bless you."

There were a couple of other partners after Sonny left, but it wasn't quite the same. They were never, ever invited to "roll over" to the other bed. It was always a kiss and goodbye.

So when people visiting my private domain eye the single beds, I am sure they wonder very simply: How did it work? What pleasure came from this frugal space? I must say it was normal and natural. I wouldn't trade the coziness and closeness of the single bed and those soft old sheets for anything.

And when I see those enormous beds people sleep in today, all I can think is how hard it must be to make them. No wonder everyone goes to the gym.

# Being Alone Doesn't Have to Be Lonely

I CONGRATULATE MYSELF THAT FINALLY, AT NINETY-SIX, I am able and willing to cope with being alone for long stretches. I smile remembering how, not long ago, I was fraught if my weekends weren't booked. There were always gatherings with friends—dinners at homes or restaurants, climbing to the upper tier of the theater, or just huddling in movie houses. A true and total New York life. In those days, I was not able to bear spending a weekend without dates in my very large apartment. Now, most weekends my greatest event is a trip to the grocery store.

I didn't use to like my own company, as I do today. It is a strange experience for me, the woman who was once terrified of isolation. In a turnabout that is almost a complete reversal itself, I often prefer solitary time.

In the apartment I feel protected by the familiar and physically free. Consequently, I do more. Being that it is also such a large apartment, there is a great deal of walking space. My bedroom to the kitchen is a good distance. Another consequence is that I don't feel cooped up. I can walk forward and back and feel I have been somewhere! How about that for being brainwashed?

Loneliness is considered an affliction of the old, but I suffered from it as a young person as well. I can reconstruct my childhood apartment, room for room, so vividly. But there are never any people in the picture—only me. Alone was the name of my sibling. As a young teenager, I wanted many friends, boys and girls, and worked very hard to maintain a large "hip" group. No matter how many parties or dates I had, I still returned home an only child, indulged and lonely.

I suspect there are very few women who are as blessed with friendships and persons in their lives like I am. There is a young woman upstairs I have known since she was six or seven years old. She loved Max Schnauzer and would visit, commuting by elevator from the eleventh floor to the seventh to play with our dog. She took me in when I had a flood in my apartment two years ago. I lived with her for two and a half months! How gracious. She continues to be a devoted companion; we discuss all the things coming and going in our lives.

These relationships blow my mind. No matter how many friends or family members one has, at some point, everyone experiences being alone. There is little to be done about that. Loneliness, on the other hand, is a condition that can creep into your being when you least suspect and must be resisted.

I am careful to keep vigil during the summer months, when the days are long and ever so lonely. I dread the heat and don't fare well in it. The season and I have never gotten along well. During the summer I was newly separated from my husband, my mother came for a visit. We walked down the middle of Park Avenue one evening and not a single car blocked our way.

During the hot, languid months, I am an outsider looking in when all seem to have summer activities that don't include a ninety-six-year-old. I turn to the mundane for help, such as cleaning or cooking for the week ahead. I keep moving, even if it's bent over the kitchen sink. If you look for things to occupy your time, you can always find something that needs your attention. It is very fulfilling to tackle and accomplish the long put-off and avoided. Then again, I really don't know the art of relaxing.

I am perhaps the only human who prefers cold gray weather in which one needs no excuse to stay home, make a soup, tidy, and curl up with a book. Summer clothes have never been my favorite mode of dressing either. Give me winter's heavy, beautiful sweaters. Or even better, fall, when designers traditionally put their best styles forward and the store is stocked with merchandise. A busy and industrious time for schoolchildren and personal shoppers alike.

I am proud of having learned to live alone. I remember when my own mother's autonomy was taken away from her. She literally gave up and took to her bed. I hold that thought as I face each new day. It took many years for me to gain enough self-worth that I could tackle the most important aspect to true independence: knowing how to ask for and accept help. This was something I always loathed, even if there was the need, because it seemed to me to show cowardice. I was wrong. Stepping-stones of assistance can be liberating and make you feel fit to move forward.

> *Loneliness is like a disease that is so difficult to treat.*

NO ONE HAS SEEN IT ALL

# What Company Radio Can Give

MY MOST IMPORTANT POSSESSION IS MY RADIO. IT HAS BEEN my best and favorite companion since childhood, back to when series, soap operas, and all sorts of entertainment were on every day. I always had my own radio, since my grandfather manufactured them. Some persons feel this strongly about television. Not I. Before television, when we were dependent on radio, one had to listen.

I am not dependent on television. In fact, I maintain strict rules around its usage. No television until after 5:00 p.m., and usually off just at 10:00 p.m., after the news. But not so the sound of the radio, which has complete freedom in my house. The radio is my third arm. A true appendage, it plays very low at all times in any room I find myself, no matter what I am doing. It is a comforting voice when I am home alone, which is all the time. Perhaps this is a quirky habit, but it is very necessary for my well-being.

The radio is even my bedtime friend. Those nights when it is so difficult to fall asleep, NPR, my favorite station, lulls me into dreamland and stays on all night for when I invariably wake and need to be re-lulled. To me, it is better than a sleeping pill.

There is something so relaxing about lying in bed, eyes closed, and listening. Many people have forgotten or don't try.

Noise does away with the fear and loneliness of total silence. I have advised so many people about what company radio can give to you.

# Independence Can't Be Bought

TONIGHT, UNDER PRESSURE FROM MY SON, I WILL VENTURE out for an early hamburger with him and his lady friend, whom I really don't know. It makes me believe that he wants me to acquaint myself with her. We shall see. I am not one to really be a huge part of my children's lives and loves. Been there, done that. I am sure I will be home in time for the eight o'clock news.

I am rather, shall we write, a different, strange mother, particularly when I look around at younger parents, which include most every parent alive today. There is a huge difference in child raising since my time. Naturally, there are similarities that defy time. In my youth, we, too, were so anxious to have children, sweet babies, all under "mommy's control." Then on to puberty, when we start losing the same—and our patience. Then the most difficult time, the teen years, when boundaries are tested and rules trampled, until they become adults and we can breathe a sigh of relief that at least we are no longer in charge.

My friends with children my grandchildren's age are doting, holding-on parents. They hold on to their adult children, be they single or married, and play a huge part in their lives. I watch, incredulous, how they are at the beck and call of grown-up men and women. From the way they turn somersaults on command, it is clear they are afraid of maintaining anything but the level of engagement you would with an actual child. What do they believe will happen? That their children will disappear from their lives altogether? Some keep buying their "kids" vacations, homes, even shopping trips to strengthen the attachment. I see this tightrope that binds parents in most every family I know.

I call myself a "strange mother" because ever since my children were little, I was determined they would grow up to be independent and strong. I was trying to right the wrongs of my own childhood that made me fearful. Looking back, I realize my mother and father held me back—overprotection, I believe it is called today. It's strange because I always wanted so much more of my mother's time when I was young, wanted her to wash my hair, take me to the park, more. I never did get it. Instead, Mother and I visited my grandmother at least three times a week. Mother saw to my nana's needs, grocery shopping, paying the cook and maid. She made her quite helpless. Mother handled me the same way. Today we would hang "control freak" around her neck.

After my daughter and son came of age, I made a huge effort to stay out of their lives, not to interfere, particularly when I am not asked or unsure of what I might say even if I were asked. My children are part of my life but a very separate part. I know how intelligent they are, so I leave them be and do not offer advice about their lives and children. I believe it is better that way, no confrontations or bad vibes. And none of it has a money connection.

Independence can't be bought; it has to be earned, and my children are very independent. Indeed, I regard them not so much as my children but adults. Now in their seventies, they are hardly "children" by any measure. However, in my book they have been fully formed adults for quite some time now. My daughter, Kathy, has had an extremely wonderful life in the art world, where she is well-known and respected. She is also a very fine writer; her intelligence leaves me often to wonder *Where did she come from?*

My son, John, never loving the big city, took himself to the Berkshires when it was still a quiet, mostly rural place. Having founded his local fire department, he subscribes to all things civic in the town where he resides. The younger of my two, he is retired. (My daughter thinks like me: retirement is not in the cards. It would be a mental disaster.) If you met him now, you would never believe John, an animal lover and well-respected member of his community, was born and bred in New York City.

My grandchildren are equally as self-sufficient as my children. I am far from your usual storybook granny. I am not always buying, calling, or baking for my three middle-aged grandchildren. The fantasy of grandchildren as a glorious time is the stuff of books. I am a pragmatic grandma. In an age when moving back in with Ma and Pa doesn't seem to hold the same stigma it once did, my grandson and twin granddaughters have struck out on their own. To me they are like the old-time workers I grew up with and understand. Most unusual as I look around today and see others.

My grandson, Henry, is an engineer and a fine baker. I guess an engineer, knowing figures, would also be good at measuring. I am not, which is why I do *not* bake. An avid biker, too, he lives in the Midwest, for which I thank the Lord. New York would not be his bag. My granddaughters, twins, are as unique as they are connected. Hannah spent two years with the Peace Corps; an accredited therapist caring for the mental health of many, she has a very big heart for such a small person. Gillian is dedicated, determined, articulate, a real businessperson on a high level. Although diverse in their professions, all three are competent and want for little. They are outdoors people and enjoy looking for the simple, good, decent things in life—much of it a throwback to my youth.

I wanted my children to be independent, but these days I wonder if I overdid it. I have never been a devotee of Mother's Day, but when creating the holiday no one seems to have taken into consideration that when your children are grown and married parents themselves, Mom falls to the bottom of the ladder. My daughter and son check in periodically and don't seem to worry about me, which is a two-edged sword. I suspect because I work a full week, they feel they do not have to be concerned. I have never relied on them, and although I am ninety-six, I still don't feel comfortable depending on them. Actually, I would rather turn to a friend for assistance or advice than burden my daughter or son. They have their own children and a great deal to contend with. This does not make me love or admire them less. On the contrary, I continue to appreciate my children more and more. Their strength makes me intensely proud.

Sometimes I do have guilty feelings and think I should be doing more, that I am not the mom I ought to be. Perhaps in my old age, I still have some growing up to do. On the other hand, it's a little late for me to become a helicopter parent.

I was prescient about my return time home from the burger date with my son and his new lady friend. I was sitting on my settee in front of the television when the nightly news began. When they dropped me off at home, I came up with a very simple thought: *I am pleased that my son seems happy and comfortable.* That is all that really matters in life and what any parent should hope for their children.

*My independence is of the utmost importance. It takes precedence over my children, work, friends. If this is stripped away, one has nothing.*

# ON AGING

# You Never Get Used to a Machine That Runs Out of Gas

IT IS ONLY ELEVEN O'CLOCK, AND ALREADY I FEEL LIKE leaving the office to go home! It has been a most anxious morning for me. The pharmacy is out of my prescription. Never has this ever happened.

I have faced the fact that I'm in my nineties. One look at the long list of my doctor appointments, and I know for sure just how old I am. I won't say it isn't frightening—the fear of illness is the worst. I am not as nimble on my feet as I was even a year ago. I'm very aware of all these everyday things that I used to take for granted—like getting dressed.

When I am in a hurry in the morning, rushing to work, and I button on my shirt, my very nimble hands don't work with the same dexterity they used to—same with tying a bow on my blouse or the laces of my sneakers. I've always been meticulous in all things regarding hair, face, and clothing. It was always easy for me, no brain surgery. I would rise each day, pull from here and there, adorn the wrists, neck, ears, put a pin in the right lapel, and be off with so little effort. My, has that begun to change. Now some mornings I find myself doing the unthinkable, standing in front of the two closets and trying to make a decision about what to wear. I like to dress for the day in two seconds—trousers, blouse, jacket, hurry. Going to work is enough of a decision! I have started occasionally putting my clothes out the night before like I did when I was a little girl preparing for the next day at school.

I guess this is when age rears its ugly head. There are other ways my routine has been changed by age. Up until relatively recently, I would arrive at the office early and immediately "run" at least three floors with great ease. I never tired of hunting for the new and exciting for people, and I am appreciative to get a phone call about what we have found specifically for them.

My running days are over. My back is turning on me. I don't put away, fold, neaten up like I used to. There's a tenuous feeling, that I am going to be ill and out of control. It isn't only my body that seems to want to give up. I misplace items in the kitchen. My memory bank skips. The easiest, most mundane things can be difficult to bring up. Names stick in the back of the brain, and I have to work hard to bring them to the fore in order to speak them. The embarrassment of others observing all this is perhaps the most difficult part to handle in daily life.

I'm aware of so much—including that this does not make for good reading—and am trying to reckon with it. I should be used to days like this, but I will absolutely *not* face the reality of my age. At ninety-six, most are headed to "the home."

Should I follow suit? Take to my bed and stare up? No, no, and more nos!

Even though my feet don't carry me as far, my age is most definitely a great asset in the workspace. People are awed at the number. They are always astounded that I still go to the office and hold down a nine-to-five job. I have never looked into the whys; I've just kept going with my daily routine. However, I guess nearly a half century in the same chair does make me an exception. Most places of business do not regard older employees as viable, let alone essential. Although my name is quite well-known in the retail world, I realize how fortunate I am in my work situation. How many companies would want the responsibility of a ninety-six-year-old?! The managerial team keeps an eye on me, but they are more concerned about my health than my business.

In my old age I have made my mind up to stay calm and move forward. Everyone has frail days, but it's important to try not to give in to them too often.

*I've learned to take one day at a time and must admit sometimes I forgot what day it was especially on Saturdays and Sundays. Old age does creep up and in!*

# I Have Celebrated Enough Birthdays

THANK YOU, LORD, ANOTHER BIRTHDAY IS OVER. OVER! I DO not like birthdays in any manner or form.

What a terrible phobia about what most persons consider a happy time. I could literally hide under the bed and never come out.

So many remember birthdays. Whether they keep books to remember, I don't know, but it always amazes me. I have guilty feelings when I receive calls, cards, packages, and flowers on my birthday since I do not keep a birthday book, mainly because of my own negative feelings.

I appreciate each gesture, but at the same time I am embarrassed by the outpouring and attention. Why is it so hard for me to realize so many people care about me? On this birthday, I was swamped with orchid plants. Someone even baked me a pie! I offer a deep heartfelt thank-you to all those who go out of their way to care for and about me. I am going to accept their attention with dignity and gratitude. I'm blessed. I know I am. Now I must believe it.

# Don't Project Too Far Ahead

IT IS A GRAY-WHITE DAY, MUCH TO MY LIKING. HAVING GROWN up in snow country, I truly relish it.

We were totally used to snowstorms and wintry days. I have happy recollections of those blizzard days when we went off to school wrapped in so many layers; the biggest problem was we could barely move our limbs. Everyone, I know, does not feel the same way I do. It has become so unusual in New York to even see snow—so I secretly love it.

As much as I would like to, at my age, I certainly can't go out and roll in the snow. Lying in bed, watching the snowflakes fall one day, I began to reflect on my age. This is a most difficult and scary thing to do to oneself. Facing reality is frightening for anyone and everyone, not only me. How do you prepare for the future? The question is large and ongoing.

I will release myself from it. People my age don't project ahead. Tomorrow is enough of a challenge. I have never been a huge planner, but at ninety-six I do not step forward much ahead in time. As I grow older, I'm appreciative of a day ahead and that I am on my feet.

# Age Has Its Advantages

A SPRING SATURDAY EVENING FOUND ME WALKING UP THE steps of a midtown club trying to locate the room holding the wedding of two young persons—one a grandchild of a very good old friend. Not so steady on my feet and worried that my stomach might give out, I arrived at the function with trepidation. However, I brainwashed myself that I would make it.

Black tie was requested, so I got myself all done up. I carefully applied makeup, which lately seems to take more time and, I might add, requires a heavier application. I put together an outfit: wide jersey pants that look like a skirt, a sequined T-shirt, and a see-through lace jacket by Libertine emblazoned with wonderful sequins and beads. I sure was dressed in beads and sequins!

The wedding was largely attended, the service quick, kind, and not without humor. Dinner was on another floor. The band played loud and clear through the hall, filled with tables on which flower arrangements towered from tall, thin vases so as not to interfere with the interaction of people sitting below them. I had a hard time wending my way through the large crowds to find my table, and not only because I kept tripping over the trousers.

The above is not an unfamiliar feeling for me. I have always suffered going to dinners, occasions, anything that has an audience of many. I harken back to childhood when, if invited to someone's home for dinner, I wouldn't find the address and instead wander around lost in a strange neighborhood.

Crowds frighten me. One would think after all the functions I have attended, including some of my own, I would be more confident. Not true at all. I feel completely inadequate. The fear of entering the premises alone can keep me from going to an event. That is one reason I don't make a fuss over anything where I'm at the center. (The other is that my family would never think of hosting anything like the wedding I attended, and I, too, find it a huge waste of the dollar.)

I have never lived within a normal head. I suffer from many fears. When I tell a friend this, they shake their head in disbelief. "Look at all you've accomplished, all the people who know who you are," they say. One has to feel these things internally.

Instead, I have come to understand that large events are not for me. The good news is that I have reached an age when I can say a very large "no thank-you!" when invited and do not feel left out or guilty. The way I live my life today, and couldn't in the past, is as a free agent. If I do not wish to attend or do something I am not comfortable with, I—in simple terms—don't do it. It is a tremendous relief to be able to be the captain of your own ship.

Being old has its advantages, but I do wish I hadn't needed to enter my nineties to accept my nature. Each of us has a way we prefer to walk through life. Some adore a crowd and a big party, and others abhor it. When you know what makes you feel comfortable and contented, embrace it, and leave the rest for those who wish to partake.

# Capture Contentment

AT NINETY-SIX I HAVE LOST HEIGHT AND BODY WEIGHT. Everything attached to me seems to have shifted or disappeared altogether. I could mourn over what has been lost but instead decided upon not caring. Life changes for all, and I have made my mind up to accept it, even encourage it, and capture what day-to-day contentment I can.

# The Youth Lifestyle Is Not for Everyone

MY EXPERIENCE AT THE DERMATOLOGIST, WHO BANDAGED a mysterious wound on my arm, was a new phenomenon for me. I had never been to an office specializing in Botox and other such treatments—let alone one as large, spacious, and modern as this. As one enters, one sees many tubes, bottles, and containers of, I suspect, supplements you may apply to face, hair, and body. I was stupefied. I also noticed the clients all looking very young—and similar. Staying young is a lifestyle. Today it is big business, as well as fashionable.

Part of me would like to know more, and yet the other side of me has no interest and rather condemns it. I harken back to my own family growing up. We couldn't have cared less about the above. The only time I ever went to a doctor for my skin was while in my teens. I had the teenage pimple problem and was sent to someone to help that.

It is strange that in knowing what I do, I don't show more interest in the "youth process." I am certain that if I knew the cost, I would develop deeper frown lines. However, what has truly kept me from any sort of procedure is my lifelong fear of physicians. Ever since childhood I have been terrified of doctors—and those were the good old days of being sick. Even when I had children, doctors would still pay house calls. I remember the physician coming in the middle of the night when I broke out with the chicken pox that I caught from Kathy in my thirties. Looking back, only now do I realize how wonderful and convenient medicine was. Anytime one is on one's own turf, one feels safer. This personalized care couldn't be more different from today, when you practically have to hand over your life's credentials before gaining entrance. It is a very bad time to have a doctor experience. The hours are sketchy. The days are narrowed down to one or two. You can go into the office feeling okay and, after the wait in the office and all the papers signed and cards presented, leave fatigued and bewildered.

It makes going to the doctor even more uncomfortable for a person already full of apprehension. No matter the reason for the visit—even a routine checkup—I begin to ruminate days before the appointment. I don't share any information with the doctor concerning my condition as I'm too busy thinking about putting my clothes on and running for it. I prefer to practice the motto *heal thyself*.

Just as I chose to wear my sweater backward as a young person, I went in the other direction vis-à-vis the youth lifestyle. I was pleased when my hair began turning gray at an early age, as I always wanted white hair à la Babe Paley. (My mother, who pleaded with me to dye it, was not quite so delighted. I think it made her feel old to have a graying daughter. As much as I liked to be the dutiful child, her entreaties fell on deaf ears; my hair has never had so much as a rinse touch it.) My best beauty advice for any age or gender is to stand erect as long as you can. Chin up and shoulders back does wonders for the appearance.

It can be difficult to face a mirror each day and witness the changes in one's facial features, even for me. But working my way down the body to my hands, a bit gnarled, crooked, cracked, awful—that is what bothers me the most. The other parts, it seems to me, we can disguise with makeup or clothing. Not so our hands, which are the most expressive part of the body. We gesture, point, use them to articulate our thoughts. I've always thought they were the most handsome part of a man. There are the great workman hands that are strong and grip tools; the slim, artistic hands of some men; and the short stubby fingers of others—these are the men I usually find suspect and to whom I don't give much time or many a look.

While I wash my face with only soap and water, if you are courageous enough to be peeled, plumped, or abraded—and that lets you hold your head up high whenever you walk into a room—by all means, indulge. I prefer a beautiful dress for the same result. However, to each their own, and their own pocketbook.

*I always wear a Necklace, or two to hide my Neck. I'm too cheap to have it fixed!*

# The Face Tells a Story

LOOKING IN THE OFFICE MIRROR TODAY—LESS FROM VANITY and more out of curiosity about my appearance in the store's bright lights—I saw what I truly look like, and it was a huge change from less than a year ago. I have a weary appearance. There are grooves on my face, not lines but grooves, and deep-rooted ones. I am not disturbed by them; I recognize my age and can handle it. However, a lot happens with the face. Be interested in what your face is trying to tell you. It has a lot to say.

# Watch Out for Signs of Boredom

"IF I AM BECOMING REPETITIVE," I TELL THOSE AROUND ME, "it is for lack of stimulation." Yes, I might repeat instructions, observations, and feelings—but isn't there a lot of repetition in daily life? If you tire of the remarks made by your elders, consider bringing new material for them to mull over.

# Sometimes You Need to Leave the Past Alone

IT WAS THE FRIDAY BEFORE THE THANKSGIVING HOLIDAY A few years ago when I stepped out of a taxi near the grocery store by my apartment. I toyed with the idea of buying a turkey breast, even though I was going to spend the holidays being hosted at the home of another.

*Go home, Betty.* That was my first thought. But no, I didn't listen to myself. Instead, I turned and went into the market and directly toward the section where I might find that damn turkey breast. Hooray! I found the last rather small one—five pounds.

So the turkey was packed up—some cranberries thrown in for good measure, because what is turkey without cranberry sauce—and off I went toward home, one block down the road. I kept shifting the heavy bag from one arm to the other, finally settling it uncomfortably on my left side. (I am left-handed.) I lugged my bird to the apartment, where the doorman greeted me with a look of confusion. "Why are you carrying such a heavy bag?" he asked. I thought nothing of it—the remark, that is.

Back in the apartment, I deposited everything in the fridge and went about making my dinner as usual. Later in the evening, though, I felt a nagging pain in my hip that continued to worsen so that by bedtime I was hanging on to the wall to navigate. Okay! You don't need a medical degree to know this was not good, but the bed felt like heaven, no pain, and I went to sleep without a problem.

Come morning, when I rose from the comfort zone, I was in real trouble. I couldn't walk without holding the wall! It was my hip. Like so many others I know, I need an operation to replace it. But in my nineties? I don't believe even the most enthusiastic healthcare consumer would go in for that—let alone one who fears any knife other than the kind you eat with.

I felt so stupid. The whole incident could have been easily avoided if I hadn't started fantasizing about Thanksgivings past. Did I really need a five-pound piece of bird? A quick answer: no. I just wanted the smell of a turkey roasting again to waft through my halls. Will I ever smarten up and leave the past alone?

I miss the turkey roasting, brussels sprouts steaming with chestnuts, and all kinds of wonderful cooking smells—not only in my large empty apartment but in the entire building, which is so ghostly quiet now during the holidays. There are no lights on. Maybe two apartments have people in them—and I'm one of them! It's a bewilderment to me. Where do they all go? When I was married and the children were young, we all gathered whether we liked it or not.

My hip was better by Thanksgiving Day, but not much better. It took a *huge* effort to dress, do my hair and face, and limp to dinner. Unfortunately, I did not know my hosts as well as I would have liked to, and certainly not well enough to cancel on them at the last minute. Although I feared that I would embarrass myself—always that fear lives within me—I mustered up the courage to gather in an apartment not far from my home.

I was picked up by my friend, who writes so beautifully and with such expertise of Japanese art. She was my connection to the host, such a tremendous collector of Japanese art that he once had a complete room at the Metropolitan Museum of Art. At the moment, his extensive collection was housed in his apartment, which incidentally was the size of a small museum itself. There were artifacts everywhere, even on the dining room table. The entire length of the table, which looked easily to seat twenty, was covered with manuscripts, pottery, papers, and books. Difficult to write about, but easier to view.

We were ushered into the enormous kitchen where we were to dine. When I saw the magnificent greenhouse attached to the kitchen, I almost flipped out. Oh, just to inhabit the greenhouse! I entertained a quick fantasy of giving up all my closets for this one glassed-in room. For my orchids alone!

When I was able to tear myself away from that gorgeous greenhouse, I immediately eyed the turkey sitting out (not covered) and cold gravy pans. It looked like dinner for many. Once seated, we were served a soup so rich, thick, and filling it could have, alone, been dinner. They hurried us to the next course like we were going to war. In between, I noticed much wine being dispersed and downed. Green beans, pies, more wine. But forget the food and so many dishes. The effort made was tremendous, and the conversation so humorous and varied, I wish I had recorded it.

I was definitely an oddity; someone they would not normally come in contact with. Everyone was so curious about what I do, how I do it, my longevity at the store. People always are. I happily answered all their questions. How fortunate I was to fill so many hours with so many interesting people of all ages, nationalities, businesses. This was a wake-up call. I have been getting a lot of them lately.

In the end, I cooked the damn turkey breast, which could have fed five. I also went off to the Hospital for Special Surgery for an injection in my left hip. Being left-handed, it would stand to reason that my left side would be the worn-out one.

Although it smelled good while roasting and like a home should, the frozen turkey and I were a big mistake from the start. *You can't go home again,* the saying goes. I was home but not the home I wanted to be in, the home from sixty years earlier. We must make peace with the home of our present and be grateful for the blessings it offers.

*Although I still suffer from youthful fears, when I do get up the NERVE to approach something new and venture into the sunset, it usually works out to my advantage.*

# Change Is Hard but Inevitable

I WAS DELIGHTED ON THE OCCASION OF OUR VERY FIRST trunk show with Libertine after the pandemic closed the store and the city. The wit of Johnson's inventive garments is matched only by their craftsmanship. It is a fun, unusual, different way of dressing. When it is shown on the floor as a collection, it can be overwhelming. However, when worn out and in a setting where the person is the only one dressed in it—it is outstanding and different and does not know an age preference (the latter being so important). Costly, yes, but a collectible. I know of what I speak; I wear his clothes often. For a party in honor of my second book, Johnson made me a custom Libertine black top with the words *Hi!* and *Buy!* embroidered in beads.

Whenever he comes to the store to present a collection to our customers, it is a cause for revelry in my book. We actually met at a trunk show of his many years ago. And for it to be the first Libertine Day after COVID had closed the city down—this was going to be a true celebration, cocktails, the works! The only vexing aspect of my dear talented friend's arrival from the West Coast was that we were only given two days' notice to contact clients! In the past, we had weeks if not months to alert people, who have very filled calendars. Upon learning of the eleventh-hour event, I had to keep myself from losing the last bit of patience I possess. For all I knew, maybe the last-minute approach would work better than the old-fashioned way of giving advance notice.

As you can read, I am not one who likes change. This character trait is a problem in today's world, where everyday habits are all in a state of flux, changing and, in some cases, disappearing altogether. Not only that, but everything is moving at such rapid speed. It's enough to give a ninety-six-year-old a complex.

At my age it can be sad to see so much of the old—both bad and good—go by the wayside, and there doesn't seem to be anything one can do about it. It isn't only technology that is disorienting. Quite a few of us are befuddled by the fact we can't call up our doctors on the phone or that normal packaged bread costs over five dollars! Never mind a roast. (I suspect I will give up meat altogether. Or buy a farm.) So many simply refuse to face the day-to-day realities when they do not suit. There is a great deal of "pulling the blanket over your head."

I want to keep an open mind to the circumstances of today. Although it may not be all that comfortable for me to endure, I believe in change. If I didn't, I wouldn't be in my business for as long as I have. Retail has always had its ups and downs for so many different reasons: the economy, the weather, wars, inflation, deflation—a virus—you name it. We are a barometer for many things happening around us and are often the first to feel their effects. From what I have learned and lived with all these forty-eight years, retail is always on the search for the New. I am not an advocate of this, for as we all know there is not a great deal of "new" in this universe.

That does not mean I favor repetition. Quite the opposite; I like to see each season bring a change in looks. What is the point of filling your closet with the same old! That is where my department comes into play, to show the clients how to buy cautiously, mix and match, add to, not too little and not too much. Healthy buying pays in the long run. However, you don't need to wear a blouse with shoulder cutouts just because it's *new*. (The cold-shoulder trend was one that mystified me for so many reasons, including its need for a painterly application of sunscreen.)

As someone who has had many lives, I'm all for reinvention. Trying to transform one's business or personal habits is more difficult than any other endeavor. I'm willing . . . if it works. In the name of keeping up with the times, I even have an Instagram account. Now, I know what you are thinking, dear reader: How does a woman who has never used a computer use Instagram? The answer is: with much assistance from assistants (another late-in-life acquisition).

Instagram has been yet another chapter in my advanced age. I try to have it come across differently, not to just finger through the clothes. Anyone can post fashions each day and say, "How beautiful." I prefer to show the workings of a boutique world, the inner regions, even the restaurant. (I'd like to get into the kitchen.) In other words, I am going on back routes and might eventually come out with the clothes. Today I journeyed through the stockroom, looking at the new receipts, touching them, explaining the process. Then we showed the stairwell down to the cafeteria, all the while steering clear of the racks of clothes. I want to stay away from what people expect of me. That has always been my focus.

Despite erroneously calling it a "blog" for a while, I have experienced some success on Instagram. I have to be prodded to post, which is something I truly don't enjoy doing as it reminds me of having my picture taken. There is nothing I dislike more than that. But I hold my breath just as I do in front of the camera; if I don't have to view myself, I'm okay with it.

I have seen from the responses that Instagram is another way to lure people to the store. I'm a believer that if enough see and hear you in any way, they will come. If only out of curiosity. The reactions are a blast. I didn't realize there are many thousands out there—somewhere—who would be interested enough to follow me. I think it's because I'm the last of a dying breed.

As long as I am able to rise from my bed, I will continue to reinvent myself. However, I am not fooling myself. There will always be certain constants. You know what I found out from Instagram? There are a lot of people like me—both men and women (the shocking part is how many men)—malcontented and scared. For us, change signifies hope. However, not radical change. You don't just turn the page over.

The Libertine trunk show was a success. Clients appeared, sipped champagne, bought embellished garments, and were entertained by Johnson's antics. It was not like the days before the virus, but then again, what is? Certainly not the holidays. One need not look farther than the first Christmas during the pandemic to understand how change is inescapable.

On Christmas Eve, I was to attend dinner with my best, oldest friend at the home of her daughter. However, when her grandson tested positive for COVID, we both decided to stay put and reach into our individual freezers. This was the first time in my ninety-plus years I spent Christmas Eve or any holiday alone! I knew I was one of the millions in the same situation and truly reckoned with the fact that it's only a day like any other. I laughed to myself. "Do I really want my son, the girls, my daughter, her son, and a dog that sheds coming over here?" Yes, I did, but it was not in the cards. So, I reconciled myself to being alone. I found a small jar of caviar in the back of the fridge and thought I might even eat it for breakfast Christmas Day! I totally brainwashed myself and my feelings.

Well, not totally. In the deafening stillness of my apartment, memories of the past ran rampant. When I was still a wife with children at home, Christmas was an undertaking the likes of which few today could imagine. We always had many persons for Christmas Eve, but to me the kitchen was the highlight, a busy warm hub of baking, simmering, and stewing.

Frieda and I would start early in December with the food:

special German potato salad with shredded bacon and dill; tiny baby artichokes (which you never see anymore) with hollandaise sauce; a wonderful, tangy herring salad, the fish from a German store; fillet of beef with mushrooms; salad with endive and all sorts of lettuces. The hors d'oeuvres table had a long wooden fish with a full Nova Scotia salmon on it looking like it had just come from the ocean, albeit with piped-in cream cheese and lemons cut to look like flowers.

From the grocery shopping to the silver that needed to be taken out and polished, there was not an idle moment. Each year the party grew, and so did the menu. The desserts had to be not just delicious but also beautiful: meringues, traditional cakes, a blitz torte. My mother would bring from Chicago hand-decorated cookies made by a wonderful woman. There were angels, Christmas trees, bells, everything in the spirit of the season. In the middle of the table was the most marvelous gingerbread house, frosted with icing to look like snow.

It was very taxing, and I must say I was always a bag of nerves: *Is this going to be right? Is it enough?* The holidays put a fear in me that can hardly be described. My lists had lists. God forbid I should forget someone or repeat a gift. It still takes me forever to choose the "right" gift for oh so many persons. I make a pact with myself every year: Cut the list! It isn't worth your nerves and anxiety. You don't have to be the most clever ninety-six-year-old on the block. They will either still like you or leave you. I never abide by what I have written.

At that time in my life, deep down I wished I could sleep through the holidays. Instead, I did the opposite. I filled tins with homemade confections, folded paper around boxes with military precision, and puffed grosgrain bows. I fussed over the table settings, the right linen, the flower arrangements—so much anxious energy put into one day without any sense of personal enjoyment or fulfillment. I could never say to myself, "Good job." Or sit at the table and enjoy the food served to me. I have missed so much in so many instances by not being contented.

That first Christmas of the pandemic, those nervous-making days were long over and gone. But not the apprehension. In the hush of my large, empty apartment, a fear that often rears its head at this stage of my life was strengthened by this new experience of spending Christmas Eve on my own—that is, the fear of being alone.

Unlike my younger self, however, I have gotten better at conquering apprehension. In other words, I have changed.

I survived the evening with a familiar mantra: *It is only a day in my life. Move forward.* Plus, I had Christmas dinner, hosted by my daughter, to look forward to. Although my family is not one that "gathers around the tree," my grandson was in town to celebrate. The virus had its own plans. Dinner at my daughter's, which started out for eight, changed to six and kept dwindling until the final tally: three! My daughter, grandson, and me.

It was a most peculiar Christmas. But I must write that in the end, it was a lovely, wonderful evening in disguise. We could talk to one another without distraction, other than the distraction provided by the mountains of food my daughter had prepared. We ate leisurely and enjoyed every mouthful. It goes to prove that even in a situation like a pandemic Christmas, we can survive and enjoy. Thankful for both, I put the experience in my memory bank.

Why is change so difficult for me? I have asked myself this question since childhood. Now that I'm in old age, I'm still asking. Throughout my entire career at the store, I've always had wonderful assistants. They stay at least two to four years then move on to better jobs. I don't fault them. My office is small and very contained—my desk and the assistant across from me. Yet when an assistant moves on, it is always a difficult adjustment for me. I don't like to let go. I had the same cleaning person for twenty-five-plus years!

One need not look farther than my kitchen to see how I avoid change like the plague. My stove—six burners, two ovens, white enamel doors—is fifty-plus years old. My father treated me to it when Sonny and I moved in, just as he did the Ecko pots and pans I still own. Daddy knew the person that owned the manufacturer on Chicago's Northwest Side. The cookware all have copper bottoms. To this day, I use them for everything, even though you have to polish the bottoms after each use! I don't mind at all.

We can never go back and must not try to replicate the past. Yet we cannot eradicate what is down deep and creeps out when we least expect it. That is why I like subtle change. From my long experience, gradual change, the kind that doesn't happen all in one thrust but that you grow with, is healthier and more lasting.

*We all, without exception, are sequestered in our own minds.*

# No One Has Seen It All

I SAT ALONE IN A SMALL COURTYARD AT THE CENTER OF A condominium community in Southampton to which I was invited by a friend for an August vacation. Fresh air, blue sky, and not a human in sight! It was so ghostly quiet, even the birds seemed afraid to sing. Not a peep did I hear.

"Where is everyone?" I wondered, looking up at the apartments' closed doors and shaded windows. Spooky for sure. The stillness, which began to creep through my entire being, made me anxious. I had come all this way to escape the loneliness of summer in the city and seemed to have fallen into the same pit.

I hear that places such as this condominium by the beach are right for persons my age. However, it took only one short day for me to figure out that, no, I don't believe so. Even if I were retired, I could never imagine myself in this situation. I am beginning to wonder if there is any place for me other than the office. There I have my window and people, interactions with persons of all kinds, all ages. There is no more tremendous benefit to my body and mind than the diversity that work brings.

When one reaches my age, one can become suspicious of what is happening in the larger world. I have never believed I have "seen it all." There is always some new thing, even if it might be the same in a different shape. This mindset is important in my line of work. I mean, how many pairs of pants can I sell and think they are all different? How many outfits can I put together that are unique?

However, finding inspiration in the mundane is so important for everyone. I can't recommend it enough. You have to train yourself, but if I can do it, anybody can. In a way, it's a search for distraction from the ups and downs of reality, and it can be found in the simplest of things. For me, a big one is what to wear when I get ready in the morning. After I rise from my bed and go through the same procedure I do for every day of my life—brush teeth, wash face, and put on a little makeup—I go into my closet and challenge myself to see the same old clothes in a different light. Then I get dressed and get out of the apartment, where I am able to treat each day as a new day, as well as a new experience.

In short, I am never bored. I won't allow it to creep into my thinking.